'A Good Eddication'

A History of Chilvers Coton Free School

David Paterson

Nuneaton 2013

Published by
Chilvers Coton Heritage Centre
Nuneaton CV11 4LU

ISBN 978-0-9927628-0-3

'A Good Eddication': A History of Chilvers Coton Free School (Nuneaton: Chilvers Coton
Heritage Centre, 2013)

Acknowledgements
Text written by David Paterson
Design by Neal Evans and Stephen Harban-Bullock, Nine Point High
Print managed by Nine Point High, Nuneaton. CV11 6RY

Images courtesy of:
John Burton: pages 22, 32, 33, 41, 45, 52, 64, 71, 72, 73, 75, 86, 89, 91, 92
Chilvers Coton Heritage Centre: pages 48, 55, 61, 65, 81
Steve Day: Cover, pages 29, 55
George Eliot Fellowship: page 53
Sally-Ann Veasey: page 82
Viscount Daventry: pages 8, 12, 13, 18, 30
Warwickshire County Record Office: pages 19, 20, 26, 27, 35, 49, 90, 94

Acknowledgements

My considerable thanks go to John Burton for his encouragement at every stage of this project and for his essential photographic assistance, locating many fascinating pictures, not least for the cover. Particular thanks are also due to Rob Everitt who helped with census research and photographs and, like John, read through a draft of the work, made helpful comments and saved me from some errors. As always, my wife Marie read through a draft of the work and also provided her expertise on census research and photography. But any imperfections of the final version are my responsibility.

I am also grateful to Carol Hughes and Carol Wright at the Coton Heritage Centre for accommodating my enquiries, providing coffee and showing me around the centre from an historical perspective. I also enjoyed a helpful chat with Don Jacques about the last days when the building was still functioning as a school. Kath Smith provided fascinating memories of the area and the school in the 1920s, a unique contribution. Thanks also to the Warwickshire County Record Office for their assistance in obtaining documents and letting me take relevant photographs from their archive. I also found useful material under Chilvers Coton in Nuneaton Library and am grateful to its staff for their assistance.

I am also indebted to Viscount Daventry for his kind permission to reproduce family photographs which enhance the human aspect of the account of the school.

Grateful thanks are also due to Steve Day who supplied some lovely postcards of Chilvers Coton at the turn of the century and also to the Warwick County Record Office who have kindly given permission to reproduce the following photographs:

1. Extract from Arbury household accounts, (payment to first School master, Ezra Evisson 1747) CR 136 V156
2. Architectural sketches and plans for the school by Sir Roger Newdigate CR 764 215
3. Codicil of Sir Roger's will relating to the school, including payment of a Schoolmaster, 1806. CR136/B7084/3
4. Plan of alterations to the school, 1874. CR136/B7084/3
5. Ground plan of school, undated [1953?]. CR136/B7084/3
6. Memorial to Lady Elizabeth Newdigate. CR 764/215

Note on spelling of Newdigate/Newdegate.

The original spelling of the name had an 'i' in the centre. After Francis Parker inherited the Newdigate estate in 1806 he changed his name to Francis Newdigate Newdegate. The change of vowel applied to the middle of the surname. Hence the 19th and 20th Century references to Newdegate use the middle e. So, for instance, CNN stands for Charles Newdigate Newdegate.

Pounds Shillings and Pence.

In the pre-decimal currency before 1971, 12 pence equalled one shilling and 20 shillings made one pound. I have kept to these old values of money as originally stated, putting their modern equivalents in brackets: so for example in Chapter One £73 19s 5d = Seventy three pounds nineteen shillings and five pence (£73.97)

What I want to give Tom is a good eddication; an eddication as'll be a bread to him.
Mr. Tulliver in Mill on the Floss

———◆•◆•◆———

The amount of knowledge Bartle Massey must possess was something so dim and vast that Bill's imagination recoiled before it: he would hardly have ventured to deny that the schoolmaster might have something to do in bringing about the regular return of daylight and the changes in the weather.
Adam Bede

———◆•◆•◆———

There was no one in the room but the nurse and the Mistress of the Free School who had come to give her help from the beginning of the change.
Amos Barton

———◆•◆•◆———

We break off a fragment from the education we suppose necessary for our own children – its mechanical and technical part – and give it to the poor man's child in charity. The inveterate prejudice, that education in any higher sense is a privilege annexed to a definite social position and graduated by it, associated itself with all our educational efforts.
Rev Henry Moseley H.M.I. 1845

Introduction

An Informal Start:
The Origins Of Education In Chilvers Coton.

'Silas had to part with her for two hours every day, that she might learn to read at the dame school, after he had vainly tried himself to guide her in that first step to learning'. [**Silas Marner**]

The manor of Chilvers Coton in North Warwickshire is an old one mentioned in Domesday Book and associated in its early history with the Sudeley family who founded the Priory of Arbury there in the late 12th Century. The 15th and early 16th Centuries had seen a variety of owners of the manor, closely associated with the adjacent property of Griff. It was all acquired – along with the former Priory lands – by the Newdigate family in 1586. The first family owner, John Newdigate, exchanged properties with Sir Edward Anderson, the latter acquiring Harefield Manor, Middlesex, as a result. The Newdigates thus acquired Arbury Hall, built by Anderson on the site of the old priory, establishing themselves as the dominant landowners in the area. John Newdigate's grandson, Sir Richard Newdigate (1644-1710) was squire of Arbury most of his adult life and his successful legal practice enabled him to acquire the adjacent manor of Astley with its castle and even buy back the old Newdigate property of Harefield. It was this Sir Richard whose innovative nature included

Sir Richard Newdigate

an interest in the education of the ordinary people of his parishes. Thus began a distinctive patrician concern for the local people, both traditional in concept yet radical in execution which lasted until the 20th Century.

When Richard Newdigate was 22 and about to get married – in late 1665 – his father settled all the family's Warwickshire lands on him, after which he resided at Arbury and was the dominant figure there for the next forty-five years. He had the inclination, opportunity and means to take a considerable and prolonged interest in Chilvers Coton and its inhabitants. He was serious-minded, strict on religious observance and a great note-maker and list compiler, taking a census of the inhabitants of Coton – an unusual move. His concern to improve the running of his estates benefited his tenants and workers on occasions. In 1687 a canal from Arbury to Nuneaton Common saved the heavy carting of water, and the construction of a great water wheel was to drain his coal mines and reduce the risk of flooding. Not all his schemes were successful. As Eileen Gooder put it in her Squire of Arbury, 'ideas, wedded to optimism, proliferated'.

Among the many evidences of concern for the people of Coton was that of an education for the poor of the parish, a largely rural one but with some coal mining, and now starting to develop ribbon weaving. Sir Richard anticipated the growing interest in schooling in the early 18th Century by a generation. The census of 1684 shows John Holmes as the parish schoolmaster living in the Heath End area of the village. He is the first Coton schoolmaster that we know about and was Master until at least 1692 (he was also Master at the Grammar School in Nuneaton in a gap between Schoolmasters around 1694-5). However, many details remain unclear. Where did the education of the Coton poor take place? At what age and for how long did children attend? Did they just learn to read – or did the instruction include writing and elementary arithmetic? Did Holmes's wife Elizabeth teach as well, so that the education included girls as well as boys? How was the teacher paid?

Answers here are speculative: there is evidence from a list of 1692 of a 'school dame', Jane Hutt. She may have been the female equivalent of Holmes or, because of the use of the word dame, (a lady who looked after very young children) as much childminder as schoolteacher, merely reading stories. This was probably in her own home as there is no indication of a school building. So, if large numbers of children attended, the parish church of All Saints was the most likely venue. Neither is there evidence (despite Eileen Gooder's best searches) of formal payment to Schoolmaster Holmes. But it is clear from slightly later evidence that Sir Richard expected large numbers of children to attend and that he would probably have paid Holmes and any female teacher. This is because in 1704 Gooder records that 'the Lord of this manor hath given a certain sum of money to Henry Simes for the teaching of poor children.'

When Simes became schoolmaster is also unclear: John Viall, born around 1665 and a graduate of St. Catharine's College Cambridge, was appointed vicar of Chilvers Coton in April 1692 and formally licensed as Schoolmaster in October 1697. Whether Simes replaced Viall or merely acted as his assistant – as Usher – is uncertain, but the latter is more likely. The Newdigate accounts for the early 18th Century show numerous payments to Viall though it is not clear if these were for teaching. There is no record of any Henry Simes being formally licensed as a teacher. This Episcopal licensing established early on the tradition of a Church of England education – a feature that continued with the more formal 18th Century school and for the rest of its existence.

The reference to Henry Simes as a teacher is in a Manor Court document relating to a penalty for parents [who] 'do refuse and neglect to send them to school'. Here again Newdigate went further than most of his contemporaries. Even if education was provided free – with Sir Richard paying the schoolmaster – poor parents were often reluctant to send their children to school for long. This was because of their earning potential from a young age, especially in an area like Coton where the growing trade of ribbon weaving afforded children opportunities of early employment; and youngsters were also sent down mines. However, Sir Richard apparently charged parents the substantial sum of five shillings if their children missed school – something that would take their offspring some time to earn. So attendance was encouraged, child labour possibly restricted and the chance for a more sustained education increased.

Vicar John Viall probably continued as a teacher in the informal school. In his Will of 1733 he left £5 to the poor of Coton and most of the rest to his wife of thirty years, Anne, although his book collection was largely lost to the area. It went to the curate in his other parish of Snelland, (north of Lincoln) his brother-in-law Thomas Parker, who is cordially mentioned in Viall's will as his 'curate and kinsman' receiving 'all my books excepting a few practical books of divinity for my wife'. As we shall see Viall's death may have been the moment, given Newdigate family developments in the early 1730s, when a more formal organisation of Coton schooling was thought appropriate.

Chapter One: A Newdigate Venture
The Establishment And Early Progress
of the School Building

'All this, you remember, happened in those dark ages..... before schoolmasters were invariably men of scrupulous integrity'. [**Mill on the Floss**]

After the death of Sir Richard Newdigate in 1710 there is no evidence that Richard, his son, wished to disturb Coton's educational arrangements. This younger Sir Richard married Elizabeth Twisden, who was

Sir Roger Newdigate

destined to play the leading role in the development of formal schooling in Coton. When Elizabeth's husband died in 1727 (predeceased by many of his children) the inheritance passed to their son Edward but on his premature death at barely 17 years old in 1734, Edward's brother, the eleventh and youngest child and seventh son, Roger, inherited the Newdigate estates at the age of 15 whilst still a pupil at Westminster school. Two years later he attended Oxford University until 1738 and then undertook the customary 'Grand Tour', finally returning in 1740. So, from 1727-39, Lady Elizabeth Newdigate controlled family business. It was her initiative that led to a formal school.

Lady Elizabeth's School is set up

Her decision came shortly after the death of Edward and the inheritance of Roger. She formalised the village's educational arrangements and constructed a local school building for the poor. How unusual was this? It could be seen as just another of the charity schools for the poor that were set up in large numbers in the early 18th Century. Some believed the common people should remain illiterate, but a consensus was growing that a basic knowledge of their Christian inheritance – particularly Biblical knowledge – was necessary. As a result charity schools grew rapidly. Over England as a whole in the mid 1730s there were over 1,400 of these schools

Lady Elizabeth Newdigate

with over 22,000 pupils. Every county was represented. By 1760 nearly half of Warwickshire parishes had set up a charity school. Reasons for action were both theoretical and practical. John Locke's writings on education around 1700 had convinced many that the young child's mind was essentially a *tabula rasa* – a blank slate – and there was a good chance of influencing it by suitable education at an early stage. Those in the Church of England were anxious to prevent the child straying from the straight and narrow religious path and so avoid the pitfalls of Roman Catholicism on the one hand and Protestant Dissent on the other. In 1699 the SPCK –Society for the Propagation of Christian Knowledge – had been instrumental in supporting the foundation of schools for the poor. This was done by individual people of varied social backgrounds but all sufficiently wealthy to present property for a school and endow sufficient income to pay for a Master or Mistress to run it. Private initiative was also common: in 1712 Richard Smith of Westminster who owned property in the parishes of Nuneaton, Hartshill and Ansley, endowed a number of charity schools in his Will including one in nearby Nuneaton, which opened in 1715. School pupils were to come from the parish of Nuneaton but this would exclude Chilvers Coton. Would Coton's potential school pupils find a home?

As well as the church and wealthy individual initiative, schools were founded by a more communal effort, subscription. One example was the preaching of charity sermons by clergymen after which a collection would be taken for a worthy cause, possibly a school. *'The charitable mob paid its guinea and crowded to the annual charity sermons to hear its generosity extolled and its investment for the next world approved'* (M.G. Jones The Charity School Movement p.12).

This method extended the social range of those who contributed to the setting up and maintenance of a charity school. The subscription school became a common feature of the educational landscape.

Schools established by wealthy landowners in their own lifetime were another way of developing charity schools; but most of these were set up by men rather than women. Chilvers Coton provides us with an interesting example of an aristocratic female initiative on charity schools. In 1733 the Vicar of Coton, John Viall, incumbent of the parish for over 40 years and probably schoolmaster for over 35, had died. The appointment of a new vicar, Joseph Wight, in September 1733 as well as the death of her own son Edward, may have led Lady Elizabeth to review the educational arrangements. The views of the new vicar are unknown but by 1736 a new curate, Oxford graduate Henry Newby, had been appointed to the parish to succeed Thomas Parker. We lack evidence to be sure that Newby was the first to teach in the new building and he moved on after two years. Certainly, however, the school was founded on the initiative of Lady Elizabeth.

It was established in 1735 'to teach 30 poor children of the parish', that is the boys in Reading, Writing and Arithmetic, the Girls in Reading, Writing, Knitting, Spinning and Sewing. This education for both sexes, but with differences in curriculum for boys and girls was typical of the time. It was advanced in the sense that, unlike previous centuries, girls' education was now seen as necessary as boys'. However, it was – on future evidence all too obviously wrongly – suspicious of the ability of girls to grapple with Arithmetic or 'casting accounts' as the subject was frequently called. The children would be expected to learn the Anglican catechism and attend Sunday Service in the parish church. This may well have led to the exclusion of Dissenters. A good deal of teaching would be centred round the Bible. The limited number suggests the children would be individually nominated, probably by Lady Elizabeth. If the pupils did well it was also possible that they would be found positions when they left, for instance in domestic service.

The Coton Free School had some distinctive characteristics. It was aimed at the poor: a difficult word to define precisely in many ages, poor was here taken to be a class of people who could not afford the small fee required for their children to attend the many schools being established in the early 18th Century which usually charged around one penny a week per child. More than this, parents of children at Coton Free School would be unable to clothe their children well and free provision of a uniform was included. Lady Elizabeth would assume these costs, as well as building expenses.

The First Building

The school was erected on land opposite the parish church, the part of the building now closest to Coton Arches. Costing £73 19s 5d (£73.97) to construct, local materials such as soft grey sandstone were used. The expenses Bills in Warwick County Record Office show that the Newdigates supplied the timber from their own manor but needed to purchase some land in order to build the school.

List of expenses from Warwick County Record Office
(reference no C21 1237)

Carpenter James Morris	£9	16s		(£9.80)
Masons, W. Hardy	£13	10s		(£13.50)
Nails			8d	(3p)
Sir Roger for timber	£8			
Mr Chaplin for board	£6	14s		(£6.70)
William Johnson, for 11,000 bricks	£6			
Robert Wilson, lime	£6	14s	6d	(£6.72)
Thomas Alexander, 6,600 tyles	£4	7s	6d	(£4.37)
John Harris, tyles		13s	8d	(68p)
R. White for stores		15s	6d	(77p)
R. Dowell Blacksmith's bill	£1	3s	3d	(£1.16)
Mr. Carter, purchase of ground	£11			
Simon Holmes, sawing	£3	4s		(£3.20)
R. Dowell another Bill	£1	13s		(£1.65)
Total Cost	£73	19s	11d	(£73.99)

The purchase of the ground from Mr. Carter is referred to in a document of 1765 (see Appendix Four) where it states that Lady Elizabeth purchased a messuage (property with land attached) which was then converted into the school. With Coton's growing population at just under 2,000 in the first census of 1801 (though only 777 in the survey of 1684) the school was aimed at the very poorest of the parish. These, classed as those requiring poor relief, would form a fair percentage of the population. *'It was settling down and having children and attempting to live on low wages or smallholdings, as well as being born to indigence, or becoming old and widowed, that put people at risk'* (A.L. Beier Poverty and Progress in Early Modern England p.213). From a later document of the 1760s it appears that Lady Elizabeth granted an annuity which produced four pounds a year. But this was barely enough even for the salary of one teacher.

Early Progress

We lack much documentary evidence of the very early progress of the school. There were always difficulties with attendance in schools of this kind and children's appearances at their desk might be intermittent and brief: there is no evidence that the older Sir Richard's imposition of a fine for non-attendance continued. Even with no fee to pay, parents saw a loss of income from children who could earn money in other ways. Farmers as a whole were the least keen on a steady education for the poor, relying on extra hands at crucial times of the farming year, work which did not require the skills of the three Rs. This may not have been quite the problem in Chilvers Coton as in some other places. The heavy clay soils of North Warwickshire meant the very young were not seen as strong enough to dig the ground and the Newdigates, keen on schooling, were a major employer in the area.

But there were other pressures on children to work rather than study. The further growth of ribbon weaving in the area in the 18th Century encouraged the employment of the young, sometimes as early as six or seven, leaving little opportunity for formal education. It would prove difficult to change this situation. Lord Mansfield, who gave a legal judgement on Nuneaton Grammar School's affairs in 1756 remarked that he had been told that small scale ribbon weavers in the area employed young children because 'they cannot afford to give wages to sons of a more advanced age'. The Newdigates were likely to have had a personal say in which children were selected for the school but may not always have been successful in enforcing attendance. Yet, unlike some others, the school continued: from records that survive from the 1740s, about 12 boys and girls a year received clothing, and a school list for 1746 records 29 children, just one short of Lady Elizabeth's total.

Sir Roger's Contribution

The school remained functional in the mid 18th Century, a time when poverty was all too apparent, the SPCK were less supportive of new school initiatives and there was a growth in child labour. Corn riots in nearby Nuneaton in 1756 emphasised the area's instability. Enclosures – which Sir Roger himself organised on his own property in 1764 – could remove the common land on which some of the poor depended to graze their animals. But Sir Roger was clearly determined to maintain and even enhance the school. The profits from his enclosure gave him the means

Sir Roger Newdigate

to do so. As Lady Elizabeth aged he assumed the family interest in the school. As early as September 1747, she was recovering from a 'troublesome illness' though she lived until September 1765. By 1763 though, approaching 80, she was clearly an invalid. In that year she wrote to Sir Roger that she was 'Greatly obliged to you for the most affectionate concern for my health which is much the same as when you left me. I found little good by any bleeding. I cannot imagine at my age that I can ever recover.'

On her death two years later Sir Roger immediately took action on the school. He was 'willing and desirous' to 'confirm the said charities' and 'to augment the same'. He re-granted the annuity of £4 to his chaplain Christopher Preston, vicar of Chilvers Coton from 1751-83, and increased it with a further annuity of £6 'to be taken from the lands allotted to him upon the late enclosures of the common fields' including Greenmoor Field and Rye Hill. The vicar was responsible

The ledger entry relating to Ezra Evisson's payment

for administering this money and paying the schoolmaster, one Ezra Evisson. Unlike the nearby Smith's Charity School which employed a Schoolmaster and a Schoolmistress with a combined (though not equal) salary of £25, Ezra seems to have been the only teacher, suggesting limited numbers. Even at £10 a year under the enhanced annuity, his salary was very low (£25-£30 annually was the average) and it is hard to see how he would have managed previously on an annual income of just £4 even with accommodation provided. While £4 is the amount paid to Ezra revealed by the accounts, later evidence from Sir Roger's Will suggests he was augmenting the Schoolmaster's salary and this may have occurred sooner rather than later.

It does seem likely that until at least the 1760s the school remained the small one that Lady Elizabeth set up in 1735, for the 30 boys and girls with just one teacher. After this, with the village developing and demand for schooling growing, Sir Roger arranged for expansion. He constructed a new set of buildings adjacent to Lady Elizabeth's school. His grand plan for a four-columned entrance was not completely followed through. Nevertheless, the frontage with a large semi-circular window did show off 'handsome stone buildings', two storeys high.

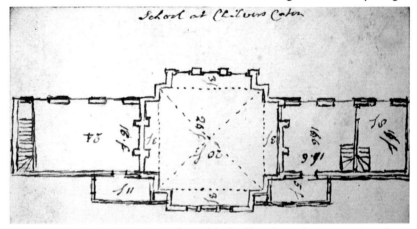

Plans of the building drawn by Sir Roger Newdigate

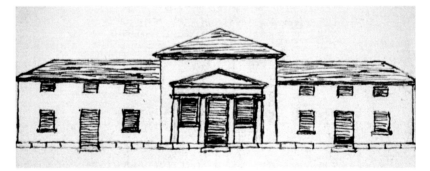

Notable features included high ceilings and tall windows. On either side of the entrance were two large schoolrooms with separate entrances for boys and girls. The Master's residence, to the right of the main entrance, had a 'good garden'. At least the endowment was not meant to include –as it often did in such cases – repairs and improvements to the building. These were also provided when required from the Newdigate coffers, one of a number of signs of how far this school development was a distinctive one, dependent as it was on the Newdigate largesse. These developments were generally supported: the accounts for this time refer to the school legacy as 'applied by the desire of the parish to the Charity school.'

While the vicar was granted the day to day administration, the Newdigates retained control of an institution set up with their money. Sir Roger and his successors were to have 'the sole and full power and liberty to displace ...the present or any future Master' and also 'at all times to put in or put out and dismiss all or any children' and to be responsible for the acts and management of the school. The vicar would be assisted by the Churchwardens and Poor Law overseers, clearly under the control of Sir Roger. Twelve girls and twelve boys, those in special need, would be clothed as well as educated. Demand was considerable and pupils were initially selected from 'settled families' from Chilvers Coton parish. Children of other residents, who had arrived more recently, would only be considered if there was room. However, Sir Roger did not feel obliged to keep the number of scholars to 30.

School expansion both in numbers and buildings could be financed by a new source of income. As Member of Parliament for Oxford University from 1751 to 1780, Sir Roger saw the value of extending the Coventry Canal to Oxford. Construction began in 1768 and the venture proved profitable for Sir Roger as a shareholder. In 1786 he opened the Griff Hollows section joining the Coventry Canal half way between Nuneaton and Coventry Communication. In his Will he left six shares of £100 each in Coventry Canal Company stock. From the dividends – which varied annually – £4 went on to the Schoolmaster, as Lady Elizabeth had previously instructed. The canal profits were partly used to finance school expenses.

The Griff Arm of the Coventry Canal, a source of income for the Newdigate Estate

The school was not entirely reliant on Newdigate finance. In 1770 the Master's salary was further augmented by £5 annual interest on the £100 legacy of Edmund Dudley, gentleman of Nuneaton, who bequeathed money to numerous good causes including the Minister and Churchwardens of Chilvers Coton on trust that they used the interest 'unto the schoolmaster of Chilvers Coton for the time being aforesaid'. Dudley left money to other parishes, two infirmaries and the poor of Nuneaton, but to Coton School rather than Nuneaton's Smith's Charity school. Was Coton in greater need? Dudley had a conditional clause that if the school closed the money should instead be distributed to the poor of the parish. But this did not need to be implemented. Sir Roger added a further £11 to make a salary of £20. Perhaps as a result, Ezra Evisson stayed as schoolmaster for at least twenty years from 1743 to 1763 and probably longer.

There is no evidence initially of a female teacher but in the 1760s Sir Roger provided one with a further £10 now set aside as salary for a Schoolmistress. The lower figure for a similar job for a female was standard practice in 18th Century charity schools catering for both boys and girls. There were Newdigate-imposed provisions: the Master and Mistress were expected to behave well, and not expect increases in pay. Sir Roger had sole charge of the appointment of the teachers and their continuation in the post, and could remove them at his discretion. Numbers had now increased to 50, all nominated by the owner: 30 boys and 20 girls. The expenses in total were between £80 and £90 annually, all met by the Newdigates.

Sir Roger showed concern for the poor and acted on information supplied by the clergy of the parish. This encompassed all young people, not just those at the school. In 1783 the new vicar of Coton, John Rennie, notified him of the ill treatment of a 14 year old apprentice by a Coton ribbon-weaver, John Clay. Sir Roger took her under his wing and looked after her for a month. Unfortunately on her return to her Master the ill-treatment continued and she died. Clay was convicted of murder, executed at Warwick and then gibbeted at Tuttle Hill in front of 4000 people.

The Coton Sunday School and the Free School

The school was indirectly affected by the Sunday school movement. As more children were employed at an early age in workshop, factory and at the loom, there was a campaign especially after 1780 to develop schooling on Sundays, the one day children would be able to attend. While religious education would naturally be a strong focus, many Sunday schools gave elementary education. Nationally there were a quarter of a million children in them by 1787 and in that year a Sunday school of this sort developed at Coton with a substantial Committee headed by Sir Roger and Bernard Gilpin Ebdell, the new vicar of Coton. Thomas Buswell and Thomas Spencer were to be Masters receiving two shillings each Sunday. It was run on a subscription and nomination system: that is a subscriber paid one guinea to nominate three children to attend the school and half a guinea to nominate one child. There were initially 30 subscribers (see Appendix Five). Since no children were to be included under the age of eight on the one hand or 'of a riper age' on the other, the target age was between eight, at which time many might be taken away from the Free School to work, and about twelve. It was partly an attempt to continue the educational work of the Free School, usually begun at five years old. If, later, they had to leave school for work, they could attend on Sundays, becoming fully literate and numerate by their teenage years, thanks to a combined effort of the Free School and the Sunday school, the latter also free to attend. The art of reading would be the first aim of such a school, with writing taught in the later years. In the 18th Century many children could do the first tolerably well but not the second.

We have more documentary evidence for the Sunday school, arrangements which may also give us a clue as to how the Free School was run during the week, probably on similar lines. In 1787 there were 82 names on roll, 50 boys and 32 girls, the odd one from Heath End and even Collycroft. There was a fairly rapid turnover, with over 20 leaving each year but with a similar number entering so that numbers were maintained. Hours were 9-4 in winter and 8-5 in summer including attendance at church and a substantial break in the middle of the day. Children were to come washed and combed 'as decently as the circumstances of their parents will allow'; some would be less than ideally turned out. Here is where the charitable giving went beyond mere instruction. 24 coats were supplied on Christmas Day 1790 and a further 18 in 1791. Sir Roger's wife nominated 17 girls for the Sunday school and conditions of attendance had to be met – seven were subsequently expelled. On the other hand there were incentives for good behaviour: twelve boys and girls received prayer books which presumably they were now considered able to read. Accounts show money spent on woollen cloth for coats, 2d per yard striped tammy for gowns, linen for shirts and coarse hemp for lining. The coats cost a total of 6s 6d to 7/- to make (c. 30-35 pence); girls received stockings. Sir Roger had a nose for needs nearby; similar material also was supplied for Sunday scholars in Bedworth, a town that roughly trebled its population in his lifetime.

The link between the School for the younger children and the Sunday school as a continuation school is shown by the lists that survive of Sunday school children in 1801 and the Free School list of the following year, unfortunately only for the boys, not the girls. 51 boys were enrolled in the Sunday school, 29 were attending the day school. The fact that there was virtually no overlap between the two confirms the idea that the Sunday school was taking boys now at work in the week. The only name on both lists, William Cox, had by far the largest number of absences in the Sunday school. Boys with under four days' absence from the Sunday school were 'rewarded' with a shirt, 35 out of 42. The most recent ones had presumably not been attending long enough to qualify for this reward. Detailed records that have survived for 1801-2 mean we can calculate attendance percentages of 96% at the Sunday school (assuming they met every Sunday) in 1802 and 91.5% at the school in 1801. These are high figures for the times and almost make one wonder if Sir Richard's late 17th Century fines for non-attendance had been revived. Charity continued, emphasising the poverty of the pupils. The list of 1801 recorded eight boys as having received shoes and a further fifteen in want of them. For many, their length of time at Sunday school was brief but for quite a number it was long enough – even on a weekly basis – to help their education along.

No. of boys	No. of years spent at school
3	7
2	5
6	4
7	3
11	2
21	1 or less

Codicil of Sir Roger Newdigate's will

The Sunday school initiatives benefited Coton Free School where numbers grew. It was not unknown for struggling charity schools to merge with a Sunday school. But in 1806 Sir Roger bequeathed an active school with a sound financial backing. How far was this expanding situation maintained by Sir Roger's successor?

Codicil of Sir Roger Newdigate's will

Francis Parker Newdegate and the Free School

Francis Parker inherited the Arbury estates on the death of Sir Roger in 1806, changing his name to Newdegate, reverting to an ancient spelling. He became well known for bringing his land agent, Robert Evans with him from his Derbyshire estates, thus ensuring Evans' youngest child and one of our greatest novelists would be born at South Farm on the Newdegate estate in 1819. But Parker Newdegate's overall reputation has not been good. This was influenced by the writer John Astley, who in his diary entry on Newdegate's death in 1835 described him as 'a dispisable character- a bad unfeeling landlord – a notorious violator of his words and promises, particularly with his tenantry'. But is this overdrawn? He maintained effectively the progress of the Free School. Near the end of his life the Charity Commissioners' report, published in 1835, but surveying the position about two years earlier, remarked that he had kept the conditions by which the school should be run, 'with great accuracy'. There was a 'liberal diet' of clothing and food. Overall, the expenditure 'exceeds the dividends on the actual [canal] shares'. Francis Parker Newdegate had clearly followed the example of Sir Roger in digging into his pockets to maintain the school and its strong charitable focus.

By the end of Francis Parker Newdegate's time there was also a schoolteacher in Astley teaching in a private house as had happened earlier in Coton. It was likely to have been for infants who could then pass on to Coton after two-three years. The first payment there was recorded in 1833.

1833: school expenditure at Coton and Astley

	Coton	Astley	
Master and Mistress	£100	£10	(Mistress only, probably part-time)
School Books, slates, rewards	£10	£3	
Coal (includes church)	£10	£5	
Repairs	£3	£5	(includes rent, probably for use of private house)
Christmas Dinner	£5	—	
Total cost	£128	£26	

In the mid 1830s just under 10% of children nationally were attending a day school but in Chilvers Coton it was considerably higher. A calculation based on the local census of 1835 and the numbers at the school suggests nearly half the children of the parish aged between five and ten may have attended around that time, if only briefly. Over 80 boys and over 60 girls was a considerable increase from the original thirty, reflecting not just the increase in Coton's population as a centre for ribbon weaving but also the growing acceptance of the importance of elementary education for all. There were intellectual challenges to the political and religious consensus of the 18th Century thrown up by the thinking of the Enlightenment in general and, by 1790, French Revolutionaries in particular. This would merely have confirmed to men of a traditional cast of mind, such as Sir Roger and his successor, the importance of instruction to children regarding the religious and political beliefs of the country in which they lived and its social conventions.

The parish was still a poor one. Sir Roger had co-ordinated other charitable gifts under the control of the vicar of the parish. The Charity Commissioners noted that nearly £294 had been spent on food and other assistance.

Vicar's charitable fund 1833

Medical (two years)	£21			
Soup	£81	0s	2d	(£81.01)
Charity Sermons	£18	18s		(£18.90)
Clothing food and books	£173	1s	7d	(£173.08)
Total	£ 293	19s	9d	(£293.98)

Also, a new workhouse was established with similar aims. As Coton vicar Gilbert Ebdell and 22 others put it when establishing a deed of settlement for the workhouse in 1802, young people that were there should be 'brought up in such habits of industry... more likely to make them useful members of society'. In 1835 Coton Free School marked its centenary and a new owner inherited it.

Chilvers Coton workhouse

Chapter Two
The Victorian School

'For to minds on the Shepperton level it is repetition, not novelty, that produces the strongest effect' [**Mr Gilfil's Love Story**]

The Years Of Charles Newdegate

Charles Newdegate's dominating presence looms over the school for half the 19th Century. Like his predecessor but one, Sir Roger, Charles inherited Arbury early, when he was 19 in 1835. Born in 1816, and great nephew of Francis Parker Newdegate, he controlled Arbury until his death in 1887. Control is also the word to describe his influence over Coton Free School. He defied many educational trends and ran the school in the way he wanted until his declining years: in the 1880s financial pressures and

Charles Newdigate Newdegate

state influence over education forced him to change his ways a little.

His Philosophy and Early Activity

Charles Newdegate combined personal charm with firm opinions. At the core of these was the question of local initiative and independence. Since the death of Sir Roger in 1806 the educational world had changed. By the 1830s few doubted the need for elementary education for the poor. Schools of all kinds, including charity schools, were springing up, especially in industrial areas, seen as in need of greater social control. Throughout Charles Newdegate's life there was a trend to restrict child labour and increase the chances for formal education by national legislation. But he always insisted on local initiative rather than central control and willingly maintained the wishes of Sir Roger. As he said a few years before he died, speaking of the school, he had 'always acted in the spirit of independence'.

Financial and administrative control of the institution remained firmly in Newdegate hands. In 1833, the total annual expenditure for Astley and Coton schools was under £150, £123 at Coton. Payments to a schoolmistress at Astley are found in both the Newdegate financial records and the Chilvers Coton School account book. The second earliest is to a Mrs. Notley in 1839-40 - one year's salary just £15, not a lot even then. Later amounts are sometimes a little larger, but sufficiently low to suggest part-time work. Payments continued until 1854 and – for a time – included some for a teacher at Heath End as well as Astley.

At Coton Free School, however, little changed in Charles Newdegate's first decade as master of Arbury. In 1845, annual expenses at the school amounted merely to £122 9s 10d, (£122 49p) with teachers' salaries at £105 taking the lion's share. Other items, including brooms, tape and cotton, were of trifling expense. Apart from the use of Bible and Prayer Book it is unlikely that money was spent on books. However, uniforms indicating charitable status continued to be paid for and worn, and expenditure included payment for the children's haircuts. Moreover, costs soon rose. The population, around two and a half thousand in the parish when Newdegate inherited, grew slightly in the next few years. Even more significantly, increasing demand for elementary education forced further change. In addition, dividends from the Newdegate canal shares were slowing down from the 1830s, as railways developed, and declined more sharply in the 1850s. Newdegate had to dig deeper into his pocket.

More Buildings and More Schools

The Centre today, The old school hall from the 1840s

In the late 1840s the first major physical alterations to the free school for 80 years were undertaken. Unlike many (though not all) other landowners with responsibility for a school, Charles Newdegate was still reluctant to accept outside financial help even from a body such as the National Society which, as early as 1817, was linked with over 1,000 Church of England schools. From his personal resources he constructed a new Infant School nearby on the other side of the road near the church. The Infant school previously held 'near the turnpike', adjacent to Coton arches, was seen as insufficient by 1844, unable to deal with growing numbers. The new one opened in 1848; it had a schoolroom of 591 square feet and 100 pupils on the register by the 1870s, the maximum allowed by its size, with an average daily attendance of 80. It continued to operate until the 1950s. Newdegate also organized the alteration and enlarging of both Sir Roger's Boys' school and the Master's house, where Schoolmaster and Schoolmistress Mr. and Mrs. Clarke resided. The changes reflected the fact that there were more boys than girls at this stage of the school's life. The central part of the building was made into a large Boys' schoolroom which probably entailed the moving of the Master's accommodation to behind the original Boys' schoolroom. His house would also occupy part of the second storey. There were clearly two separate schools, Boys' and Girls'.

Charles Newdegate continued to support the schoolteacher at Astley and, at first, the similar infant teaching at Heath End run in the 1840s by Mary Howe. Like Astley, Heath End School was in a private house as a development of one of several dame schools then operating in Coton parish. However, accounts show Mary Howe's payments stopped at the time the new Infant School was planned, though she continued to take pupils. At first Newdegate wanted these infants to attend his new school but in 1857 changed his mind and organised the construction of a school building at Heath End. This was superficially so that the Infants there, probably under seven,

Charles Newdegate

would not have to travel too far and it was becoming increasingly common to develop separate schools for the 5-7 age group. But his decision was also influenced by the fact that the Roman Catholics were considering offering free education in the area, which concerned the anti-catholic Newdegate: since 1840 there had been a Roman Catholic school in Coton Road.

Heath End School was erected on glebe land by local subscription assisted by a grant from the Committee of the Privy Council on Education, Newdegate's first acceptance of outside money. With an area of 540 square feet it had accommodation for 68 children. By the 1870s space was tight with 88 children on roll though with an average attendance of 60 they could just manage. Mary Howe had taken up the teaching reins again in 1857 but had retired by 1861. The school progressed as an Infant School from which the young pupils could pass to the Boys' or Girls' school at Coton. But for it to be viable a fee of 1d a week had to be charged. In contrast, the main school in Coton remained free even though by this time the majority of schools of this kind had resorted to charging 'school pence'. However, rising expenses meant that Newdegate was eventually forced to accept assistance from the National Society in the mid 1860s. Once outside money was taken he also had to accept inspection from the local diocese (Worcester) to ensure that it was being well spent. Ideally, he needed to get his teachers qualified - certificated. This could mean new staff who had undergone a course of full-time training, but also existing staff who could become certificated by further study and passing an external examination. It took many years for all Coton's teachers to become certificated.

Financial Pressures Mount: More Building Undertaken

Money was not merely required for buildings. By 1863, the annual Free School expenses had risen by about £100 in thirty years to £242 15s 6d (£242 -77p) with about £220 on salaries, as more teachers or assistants were required. The rest was spent on 'Sundries'. At the Boys' school a pupil teacher was employed to assist the Schoolmaster after 1865. This produced a further strain on the family resources but after the Education Act of 1870 Newdegate was even keener to keep his schools as independent as possible. He saw the new locally organised Board Schools, set up all over the country as a result of the Act (300 in 1870/1 alone), as the most expensive form of education, financed through a special local rate. According to the Act religious education in these schools was not to be 'distinctive of any particular religious denomination'. Newdegate saw this as potentially weakening the position of the Church of England and felt all the more determined to oppose their establishment in the area. With a good range of church schools, both Nuneaton and Bedworth parishes resisted the introduction of school boards and Newdegate was determined to do the same for Chilvers Coton. But going it alone was increasingly difficult. Without money from rates it was hard to find enough to spend on school facilities merely from National Society grants. So, the amount supplied from private sources by Newdegate continued to increase. In 1871 the construction of a specific building formalised teaching at Astley, adding further to his expenses.

By 1874 there were growing numbers of children now attending school, ncar universal in the five-nine age group. So Newdegate felt obliged

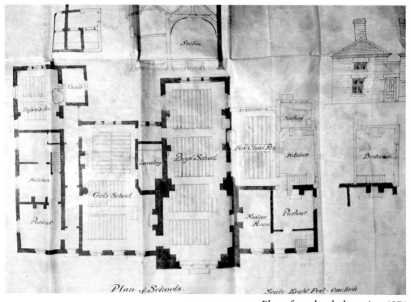

Plans for school alteration 1874

to improve the Girls' school in the way he had the Boys' one 30 years earlier. Gone were the days of the husband/wife schoolteaching team so this change included adapting Lady Elizabeth's original building for separate accommodation for the Schoolmistress. There would also be small enclosed play areas for boys and girls at the front of the building, increasingly expected in schools. A partitioning of the schoolrooms would enable more flexible teaching of larger numbers. However, the principle of a large schoolroom at the heart of the teaching still prevailed. The changes had been modest and they proved barely sufficient.

In 1881 increased financial pressure caused Newdegate to decide on two innovations: to introduce a small charge for pupils (while allowing a handful of the poorest to be excused) and to let the growing Infant school be moved to the schoolroom at the vicarage premises, thus passing it into the hands of the community. His last years were proving even more financially strenuous for him with the fading of the old system of aristocratic control. Charles Newdegate's successor, his cousin Sir Edward Newdegate, initially increased the number of children excused payment (see below). But after 1891, with only limited exceptions for schools already charging high fees, no payments could be levied in elementary schools receiving grants. So the school reverted to its free for all status. Up to 1881 when – in contrast to the school in adjacent Nuneaton – there were no fees, some children had been attracted from the north end of Edward Street, near Nuneaton town centre but located in Coton parish. Now, faced with a fee similar to the Nuneaton schools, they left the 'Free School' as 'they think it [Vicarage Street school] nearer'.

The School and the Church

In retaining control for as long as they did, the Newdegates ensured the school remained a Church of England one. In many schools the Payments by Results scheme (see below) had increased time spent on the 3Rs, partly at the expense of religious instruction. However, at Coton there was a regular diocesan inspection on the knowledge of the Catechism, Bible, Christian year and Prayer Book. Vicars of

Coton regularly visited the schools and the sudden death of one of them, George R. Pennington in 1883 (who died in church shortly after delivering a sermon), resulted in them being closed a few days later for his funeral.

The close relationship with the Church continued. Right through the 19th Century there was a day off school for the Sunday school treat. One of the schools could even be closed for a day when an important church function was held on the premises. The Reverend Robert Chadwick, who replaced Pennington, took a keen interest in the school in Charles Newdegate's declining years. After the latter's death in 1887, Chadwick exerted the main managerial control of the school, with a benign but less direct interest from Charles' successor, Sir Edward Newdegate (see below). Vicar Chadwick was also in charge of the Infant School now held in the Vicarage schoolroom. In the past the aim of the two schools had been to turn out well-behaved Christian young people rather than seek a paper qualification which – in the early part of the century – had been of little interest to employers in mines and owners of looms. These entrepreneurs had not originally demanded much of the knowledge or many of the skills the children might have acquired at school. However, railway and other industrial development, especially in neighbouring Nuneaton, as well as the growth of clerical employment, now led to a demand for greater levels of literacy from school leavers.

Staff Development

Early school development had been undertaken with remarkably few teachers. Up until the 1840s it was common to teach the pupils in the large schoolroom, one for boys and one for girls, assembling in their respective accommodation with just one schoolmaster and one schoolmistress. The aim would be to get scholars reading and counting; writing would come later. There was a tendency to rote learning: a monitor would read out words aloud and then write them down and the children would copy. After 1846 a pupil teacher scheme developed nationally whereby the most promising of these monitors – the quickest learners in the school – would train to become proficient teachers. Newdegate did not initially take advantage of this opportunity but in the 1860s a Mr. Lawrance was employed under the scheme. This kind of teacher remained throughout the century and monitor numbers faded. But change at Coton was gradual: as late as 1894, two young men were employed as 'temporary monitors'. Writing was now taught at the same time as reading.

Teachers could have long careers, starting very young and continuing to a considerable age in a time without pensions. In 1841 Ann Morris, 65, was living next door to the School House and may already have been the Schoolmistress at the Girls' school for some years. In contrast the occupant of the school house was the young 20 year old John Auld, a north-easterner, who seems to have had charge of the Boys' school. Auld later became a professor of dancing and a musician back in his native north-east and must have seen his post as a stepping-stone to greater things. He was soon replaced by John Clarke who had begun his career as an Usher – assistant Master – at Fillongley School but then became Master at Coton, with his wife Headmistress of the Girls' school, a common arrangement. A mid-career change to teaching was also possible as shown by an interesting appointment in about 1848. Thomas Robinson had, until 50 years of age been a baker in New Milverton near Leamington but was then appointed Astley schoolmaster, staying until his death in 1865 (see Appendix Two for list of head teachers).

If the schoolmistress was not married to the schoolmaster she was frequently unmarried, like Mary Howe at Astley; this was starting to be a career route for single women. There was pressure on staff: when teachers left they were not always replaced quickly. Thus in 1877 when an assistant Master left the boys school, two monitors were appointed from the top class to replace him. Another full time teacher did not appear for several months. Occasionally we find teachers from Lincolnshire. Charles Newdegate's mother's family – the Boucherett's – owned a family property in that county at North Willingham and promising teacher material could be selected from here as well as the Newdegate's other property in Harefield. Local Coton talent was also sought. Thus, Willliam Hobley, a young 18 year old cordwainer in 1851, was appointed by 1856 to be an assistant to the Boys' schoolmaster, John Clarke. By 1861 he was acting for Newdegate in his colliery business and ten years later was his private secretary. He was to marry widow Ellen Mottram whose daughter Ellen would later become Headmistress of Coton Girls' School.

Changes In The School From The 1870s

In the 1860s, once outside money had been accepted, the payment by results system introduced by the national Revised Code of 1862 affected the school until the 1890s. Grants were based on the number of children attending and their performance in the three Rs. Children were assessed at a 'Standard': there were six of them, one being the lowest and six the highest until a seventh standard was added in 1882 (see Appendix Eight). Pupils would move at different speeds through the standards and so classes could be mixed in age. Some children would not stay long enough to progress very far. For instance when Coton pupils were examined in Standard two in Arithmetic in 1872 – multiplication by simple numbers – 'nearly all failed'. Grants would depend on a combination of pupil achievement and good attendance levels: elementary schools had previously felt obliged to limit their curriculum to the basics. But then the Education Act of 1870 had a considerable effect on all existing charity schools. The curriculum widened, attendance levels rose, staff numbers increased and more buildings were frequently required. All of these changes could be seen in Coton.

The Curriculum

The traditional ingredients of elementary schooling for the poor were religious knowledge, reading, writing, and 'casting accounts', as well as needlework for girls. But in the 1870s and 1880s the idea that children of working people were only entitled to a basic education in the three Rs was being challenged. From 1875, under the Revised Code, good performances in additional subjects by individual children would qualify the school for extra payments. Pupils who reached Standard four now had the chance of widening their horizons. In the Girls' School in 1876/7, as well as traditional dictation and grammar, there was geography and music, and, by 1881, woodwork and history. In September 1885 a trip was organised to Charnwood Forest, the first of many outings. In 1887 pupils learnt about the geography of Italy and the 'mood, tense and agreement of verbs with their subject'. The first signs of science teaching came from the Boys' School in 1891 when animal physiology was taught. In 1893 there was 'singing by the ear' and visitors were regularly entertained with a song. From 1871 military drill was introduced in both schools as a result of the revisions to the national education code. Seen as good for both discipline and health it was given by Sergeant Cooper who also taught it at Nuneaton Grammar School. There was some praise from inspectors; for instance in 1890 pupils' drawing was commended. Geography was 'taught with considerable success' it was reported in 1899. Religious education could slide over into moral education more generally such as the talk in 1898 on 'Alcohol – and its effects on food'. In 1899 the school benefited from receiving an elementary school science grant. Three years earlier 'a very nice young man' had brought samples with him from the Beehive Wool Company to show the pupils.

Coton may have been in spirit a private charity school but they were benefiting from improvements to schooling that were occurring in the early period of mass education after 1870. Expectations were raised,

Pupils from Wembrook Primary School re-enacting lessons

attendance officers would inspect registers, factory and employment legislation further restricted child labour and compulsion gradually overtook elementary education. Teacher training developed in sophistication and the profession became more qualified. Children's surroundings improved and they attended more often, more continuously and to a greater age, especially in the crucial area of 10-12 years old. Their achievements would become greater. Employment, requiring more academic skills in reading and writing, was growing for both boys and girls in areas such as clerical work and, later, typing.

Discipline and Attendance

In October 1883 discipline was reported as 'pretty good'. The log book records the odd measure of chastisement. Since at least the 1830s and possibly earlier the school had encouraged good behaviour with 'rewards' and taken a moderate view of corporal punishment describing it as 'economised', meaning it was only used for more serious offences. This was not unusual: the National Society discouraged corporal punishment. The cautious policy was maintained: caning was not normally used merely for poor work, girls being kept in at lunch time. But, in 1878, when one girl had still failed to learn her lesson the Headmistress reported 'I boxed her ears and sent her home.' Her Mother brought her back and was 'very insulting'. However, her Father came in later and 'acknowledged the fault.' Girls who had been rude were ordered to sweep the school.

The boys were not angels either: in January 1885 Mr. Hales, Churchwarden, complained to the Headmaster that the Congregation could not attend the Church without being disturbed by the boys' unruly conduct which during one service had been 'most disgraceful'. At the boys school in 1887 a boy was caned for being rude to the caretaker. In 1893 several boys suffered the same fate for killing young birds in the dinner hour and there were truants who were caught. In 1898 one boy had a whip removed after striking another boy and then had a severe attack of hysteria which resulted in him being kept off school. Misbehaviour in the Churchyard on a Sunday was a problem. Positive rewards for behaviour and achievement were common. In 1890 six boys were given medals for 100% attendance over the year and in 1895 there were 26 prize winners. Prizes went back at least to 1882, originally to encourage attendance; in 1885 several were received at Coventry from the Archdeacon.

However, regular attendance of all scholars remained an elusive goal. In the mid 19th Century pupils would rarely stay more than about two years often leaving by the age of nine or ten to enter the weaving trade, or sometimes the mines. Even while at school their attendance was not necessarily consistent. After 1870 and especially 1880, when attendance became compulsory nationally, it remained hard to enforce. After 1880 it was common for children between 10 and 14 to leave when they had attained Standard four. While 156 boys were on the roll in 1892 the average attendance was 120, the best boy attending 418 out of 420 sessions. The problem had continued right through the century. In January 1892 a school attendance meeting in Nuneaton looked at average attendances in surrounding areas: Coton Free School was the lowest.

Special educational needs had no special treatment. In October 1887 one pupil was regarded as 'almost an imbecile' because of a childhood accident. Another problem was half time working, allowed between the ages of 11 and 13. The school had a high percentage of these scholars and inspectors noted it would be difficult for the school to improve further if this situation remained. In 1896, 18 boys applied for a labour certificate and so ended their formal education aged 11. Bad behaviour or poor attendance could be reasons for refusing this privilege. A pupil from another parish could be excluded but not from Chilvers Coton. As a result, in May 1897, one boy who used bad language and hurled stones at the school windows was removed since 'as he resides at Stockingford he will not be admitted again'. (For this boy's previous adventure see Appendix Six).

The school was disappointed with the local school attendance officer, first appointed as a result of the 1876 Education Act. In 1887 the head reported that this man had made 'no effort' to reduce absences. This was a common problem as many officers, initially appointed by Poor Law Guardians, were under pressure from local employers, desirous of cheap child labour. In addition, the long lunch break took its toll. As a random example, on 18th April 1896 there were 135 boys present in the morning but only 126 in the afternoon. Some poor children, if they got very wet on the lunchtime journey, had no other decent clothing to change into and so would stay at home.

Illness and poverty
Illness, poverty and unsupportive home backgrounds remained. Some

educational change evolved slowly: in rural areas school attendance at harvest time was always a problem. Coton was enough of a mixed area to be affected by this. 'Many children about in the fields' commented the Girls Logbook for 7th September 1877 and again in 1880 and 1883 'several children were away gleaning'. As late as September 1889 this was recorded in the Boys' School Logbook. A new reason for the odd day off was modern large scale circus entertainment that was spreading in the late 19th Century as working class leisure time and pay packets increased. There was a holiday for Barnum's circus in 1889, Sanger's in 1895 and also in 1904 for the local appearance of Buffalo Bill.

As regards the health of the pupils, there were serious outbreaks of illness in the Girls' school: ringworm 1879, measles 1884 and 1896, scarlet fever 1890 and 1895, and flu 1897. In the Boys' school there was measles 1875, scarletina 1876, (when both schools were closed) measles again 1885 with 47 absent, ringworm 1889, and several cases of typhoid. One boy died of fever in 1891. Illness also took its toll of the teachers in the Girls' school. Susannah Nicholas, appointed in 1875, was said by the middle of 1876 to have 'raised the condition of the school' but by the autumn of that year she was seriously ill and died on December 19th. Her successor Sarah Gee was similarly conscientious – and similarly afflicted. She taught at Heath End from 1873 to the end of 1876 before moving to the free school. Inspectors soon reported that she had 'proved her desire to maintain a high standard of tone and efficiency' and 'has taught her scholars intelligently and successfully.' But ill health then overtook her. Still, her sudden collapse and death on Crewe station in August 1888, on her way back from a holiday on the Isle of Man, was unexpected. She was only 47. Her successor Ellen Mottram remarked in 1888 that 'I find the work of the school generally deficient. This is in a great measure due to the failing health of the late Headmistress.' Things were soon back on track but this time illness produced resignation rather than death and its link to school work was clear. In May 1897 Mottram resigned because of strain of work, in particular laryngitis.

In the Boys' school there were similar problems. Teacher stress in the 19th Century was just as common as in later times. Thus Mr. Woodward arrived at the Boys' school in 1896. After a month's trial in which he gave 'much satisfaction' he was taken on but within a few more weeks was suffering from 'nervous derangement'. He attempted to return on a couple of occasions but never fully recovered.

Ellen Mottram's Gravestone

Thomas Robinson, Headmaster from 1870 to 1887, seems to have survived without much ill-health. Son of the former master at Astley he was an experienced teacher having assisted his father and then taught at Arley. However, inspectors reported in 1878 that he was over-worked and needed an adult, or two extra monitors, to assist him.

The Implications of Growing Numbers

School numbers were more than maintained. The proposed closure of Smith's Charity school in Nuneaton, first mooted around 1892, might have suggested that a private charity school would struggle in the days of free education but, with a rapidly growing population, and fewer schools than in nearby Nuneaton, Coton Free School was full to bursting. The school was adapting to become a more general elementary school for a growing area. Demand for places remained great. More teachers were now required in the Girls' school. In 1872 there had been just 48 pupils but in the decade when elementary education in England was transformed, this climbed dramatically to 76 by 1879. As late as June 1882 Schoolmistress Sarah Gee bewailed 'I am without assistants' since her monitorial helpers had left, though later in the year a full time assistant was appointed. This was just in time as numbers now rose rapidly again. By 1897 over one hundred girls were attending and there were just three full time staff and some monitorial helpers. With a large hall and one classroom, groups had to be taught at either end of the hall, hardly an ideal arrangement. In 1898 an Inspector reported that 'the main room is very dark'. Further expansion and alterations were required. In November 1896 the intake coming from the Infant school to the Boys' school was delayed two weeks because a teacher had just resigned and a replacement had not yet been made.

Inspectors and teachers

Inspectors were generally positive about the efforts of staff. At the Girls' school in 1874 they were 'carefully and thoroughly prepared' and in 1881 the diocesan inspector was 'very satisfied'. In 1887 the school was raised to the first class and in 1893 it was regarded as a 'thoroughly good school' with 'pleasing application'. In the Boys' school an Inspector of 1875 reported they showed 'considerable intelligence' but, though Mr. Robinson had 'worked hard', their expression could be 'more articulate'. This reflected the mechanical approach to teaching encouraged by the Payment by Results system. In 1879, however, Mr. Robinson was congratulated on the boys' 'achievement and tone'. He was working from a low base. Some children who had come from the Infant School had learnt little: The forty in Standard 1 could 'scarcely set down units and twos correctly'.

In the early and middle years of Charles Newdegate's time all the Coton teachers had remained unqualified, though about 40% in the country as a whole had obtained a certificate by 1870. So, at Coton, pressures grew to receive trained teachers and some existing ones became certificated.

Miss Elizabeth Cross, who taught at the Girls' school between 1882 and 1888, went to Birmingham in December 1883 to be examined for her qualification. Others left for full time study to enter Saltley Training College such as Mr Sage in 1888 and Walter Cox in 1895. By the early 1890s staff numbers were growing. They were increasingly likely to get a classroom of their own and teach a variety of subjects. The more rigid methods of the payments by results era were fading.

Furnishings and Fees

Having to make your voice heard in a large schoolroom had long-term effects and emphasised the need for more classrooms and a different approach to the management and organisation of the school. It was soon to come. The widening curriculum, increasing numbers and higher standards expected of school buildings forced further changes. Large schoolrooms could be divided and at Coton the number of individual teachers at the three schools increased. The Girls' school expansion of the 1870s had put their buildings at a higher standard than the boys. An inspection of 1891 remarked that lighting and ventilation were better than in the Boys' school: 'The girls have a much more comfortable provision than the boys'. But even here there was a constant pressure on space.

The Boys' school was now feeling its age. In 1881 it was 'whitewashed and coloured' but more substantial changes had to wait. In October 1883 the floor was described as being 'of brick and very cold in winter'. For some time, more and more schools had been getting wooden floors. In Coton they finally arrived in 1884 and were soon reported to be 'much more comfortable'. The following year eight more desks appeared. On his arrival in 1887 new Head George Mosedale had the blackboards renovated but in 1890 the lighting was reported to be 'hardly sufficient'. In that year, however, the ventilation was improved with three new large air outlets to stop the down draught. Gas fittings were planned.

Children near the school

In June 1887, two months after Charles Newdegate's death, his successor, Major-General Sir Edward Newdegate, formally visited the school with his wife. He ordered that more pupils from poor homes receive exemption from the fees imposed six years earlier. In the Girls' school this would apply to 18 children rather than 12. But the days of school

A girls' class Edwardian times

fees were about to disappear in most schools with the implementation of the Free Education Act in 1891. In lieu, an increased grant of £93 18s 6d (£93 92p) was obtained by Coton: the management would now find all copy books, slates, exercise books and any other educational equipment from their grant. Up to the end of the century Worcester diocese continued to assist with an annual allowance to raise salaries of assistants, £10 by the end of the century. The Newdegates were still responsible for the maintenance of the building and new classrooms were first considered by Sir Edward Newdegate on a visit to the school in 1892. He now planned further changes to the buildings. But Voluntary Schools like Coton, though in receipt of central government grants, could not receive money from local rates as could the expanding Board schools in other areas. The alterations were to be largely financed as well as arranged by Sir Edward.

An early photograph of the School

Chapter Three:
Forty Years Onwards
The Transformation Of Education In Coton, 1893-1932

'He might save himself a great deal of labour and expense if he could learn to read, and so he had begun to give his spare hours to the night-school, resolving that his "little chap" should lose no time in coming to Mr. Massey's day-school as soon as he was old enough.' [**Adam Bede**]

If the 25 years after 1870 had produced considerable change at the school, this sense of alteration accelerated from the 1890s. By the end of the century there were 240 pupils at Coton, 131 boys maintaining their customary numerical lead over 109 girls. There also remained a discrepancy, typical of the times, between the salary of the Master and Mistress, with annual salaries of £130 and £80 respectively, not as high as many Head Teachers elsewhere. The extra numbers without extra teachers produced problems. In September 1899, 84 girls in Standards one and two had to be taught for a while single-handed by the Headmistress. Three years earlier inspectors reported that Miss Mottram 'must find it a very difficult task to manage her crowded school with only the minimum staff required by the task.' No wonder she suffered from laryngitis.

More Building Alterations

So, by 1893 building improvements were urgently needed. 'The scullery and portions of the Schoolmasters' House required for the new addition were taken down and cleared'. There were new drains, fireplaces, chimney stacks and windows. 'Best quality local stone' was to be used. In the Boys' school new classrooms were created including turning the rest of the schoolmaster's house into a classroom. This was typical of many schools at this time: pressure on space for classrooms frequently meant the end of the guaranteed accommodation that had previously gone with the job. For George Mosedale this was not inconvenient. He was married on the 31st July 1893 to Coventry girl Emily Pears and by 1901 –and probably before – was living in Fitton Street. He almost certainly moved house when he married.

The Boys' and Girls' schools, however, remained firmly separate with different entrances. Only the noise at playtime from the separate playground would betray the existence of the opposite sex. In the Girls' school an extra classroom was erected and a small library started, reminding us that the expanding curriculum and different ways of teaching were driving the changes to the buildings. In September 1893 it was noted that 'the new classrooms are a great addition'. Coton now became, like many other older elementary schools, one where the old schoolroom was still dominant but where there were some limited moves to a different system of individual classrooms. By this time the Girls' School had four members of staff, all young, and only one with qualifications. At this time it was noted that more office accommodation was required. In 1899 a separate water supply for the school was planned and in 1901 part of the playground was paved, emphasising the greater importance now given to exercise in school. Yet despite these improvements the increasing numbers meant that, by 1901, the accommodation was again seen as insufficient as growing numbers pressed ever more on resources.

The Newdegate Link

The Newdegate family continued to make personal appearances, and annual invitations to Arbury continued through the 1890s. Lady Newdegate brought in blue woollen cloaks for the girls who had excellent attendance. In 1900 she paid a visit to examine the needlework. After Sir Edward's death in 1903 the Newdegate link continued under his successor, Major General Sir Francis Newdegate. But it was to become just that, a financial connection rather than the absolute control and ownership of his predecessors. Sir Francis maintained a patrician interest, presenting prizes and awarding the occasional half-day holiday.

In all schools of Coton's type, grants were replacing fees as the main form of finance, not that Coton's fee-paying phase had lasted long. But this would put additional pressure on the Newdegates as even the determined Charles Newdegate had acknowledged back in 1881. As a result the school's income became boosted by a subscription system organised by local worthies. In suggesting a method that had already been used for money-raising in the

Edward Melly

Infants' School, Edward Melly argued that it was only just, since 'it [was] manifestly unfair that the whole burden should fall on one person' [Newdegate]. By the end of September 1894 over £37 had been raised from 20 subscribers and by 1899 over £90 from 33 subscribers (see Appendix Seven). The aim may have been to keep board schools at bay: but the development was very late in the day compared with many other places. With increasing state aid the subscriptions would soon dwindle in the early part of the next century though not completely die out. Up to the 1930s small payments from about fifteen to twenty people continued but the giving was now nominal, raising just £3-£4 in total.

Changes in administration paralleled changes in finance. The school had been distinctive in Charles Newdegate's time for being run by him on a personal basis rather than the usual scheme of a small group of school managers who, in many other schools, administered the distribution and spending of the grant and kept a watchful eye over school standards: they needed to bear in mind the increasing frequency of inspections after 1870. Newdegate had employed his principal agent, Isaac Evans (brother of George Eliot) and later Isaac's son, Walter Pearson Evans, to do the necessary administrative work. After Charles

Isaac Evans

Newdegate's death, we have seen that Coton vicar Robert Chadwick developed a close connection with the institution as a school manager. Other local subscribers such as mining contractor Edward Melly and builder Thomas Smith became managers and occasionally presented prizes. Certificates were granted for regular appearance and more impartial Attendance Officers appeared from about 1893. A combination of these officials, restrictions on child labour, higher parental aspirations and strong teacher commitment produced a more consistent and long-lasting schooling for many girls and boys. Numbers also increased partly because the school leaving age was raised to eleven in 1893 and twelve in 1899.

Still a Voluntary School

Administratively, the future of the school lay with what was happening in nearby Nuneaton. Chilvers Coton was in danger of being dominated by its fast-growing near neighbour: as James Knox remarked in 1894, 'Nuneaton and Coton are now so interlinked that whatever happens to one will affect the other.' In 1893 Nuneaton, Coton and Weddington had formed an Urban District Council but Nuneaton and Coton still resisted the idea of having any Board School. These had grown since 1870 to a point where they educated nearly half of England's elementary schoolchildren. Voluntary schools like Coton were struggling to find the financial resources necessary to keep up. The result was that local pride in independence was now producing shortage and overcrowding. A common alternative view, especially among Nonconformists, was that schools like Coton should change their status. In April 1899 at a meeting of the Nuneaton Education League, pressing for more Board Schools, local builder Alfred Bedingham complained that the Church of England was not serving children well 'keeping them in crowded schools'. This criticism would strike home in Coton. A resolution to accept a school board was passed unanimously. Congregational Minister Reverend John Gascoigne argued for 'an education free from religious or political bias'. The rapidly increasing population of the area – from 15,000 to nearly 30,000 from the early to the late 1890s, he claimed, meant that though 'the artisans of Nuneaton were entitled to the very best', 500-1000 additional school places were now required. Three to five year olds were now seriously neglected. Religious division often remained at its bitterest over education. Guest speaker Rev. J. Hirst Hollowell, a Congregationalist, and Secretary of the Northern Counties Education League, argued that the catechism (that all Coton children would be taught) was 'one of the most horrible statements ever written'. Recent grants from the Government had given Coton School £85 with Heath End receiving £20 and the Infant school £55. This was 'the first time in English history that the taxes had been handed to a Bishop from whose fingers they filtered into the voluntary schools' [such as Coton], thundered Hollowell, a leading national figure in Nonconformist agitation over education.

However, while these demands were resisted, the insistence on local pride maintaining voluntary schools led to the failure to deal with local overcrowding. The Girls' School logbook of 1903 recorded that there were 182 girls on average in attendance, strictly more than for the space available, and additional staff were needed so that the Headmistress

Chilvers Coton Infant School

A class from Chilvers Coton School. Note the pupil teacher on the right hand side

had more opportunity to exercise general supervision. Two years earlier a report on the Boys' school argued that accommodation was now 'insufficient.' In 1904 both schools were reported as requiring additional classrooms. In February 1905 the number of boys on roll reached 200: on the basis of the 10 square foot per pupil rule the maximum number of children should have been 152: even with absentees there were usually around 170-180. In 1914 an Education Board missive warned that the accommodation limit for the two schools must not be exceeded, but war then intervened. By early 1915, 29 out of 156 girls were over twelve, a higher proportion than hitherto, with one over fourteen.

Changes in administration

The debate on whether schools like Coton should become Board schools was soon outdated. Under the Education Act of 1902 school boards were abolished and urban districts over 20,000 were to be responsible for elementary education in their areas. On May 1st 1903 the new Local Education Committee assumed its new responsibilities with regard to Coton. Could the cost of further development of the buildings now come from local government assistance? It was not to be. A voluntary Church of England institution, Coton Free School became a denominational 'non-provided' school, one of 14,000 in the country. This meant that money from the rates would finance its day to day running and its teachers' salaries. However, the capital sums required for substantial changes to the buildings still needed to come from the Church or in Coton's case the Newdegates, even if normal 'wear and tear' expenses would be met by the local authority. The Church of England would continue to organise religious instruction, much to the anger of Nonconformists. They were hardly mollified by the continuation of a conscience clause, begun in 1870, allowing parents to withdraw their children from Anglican religious teaching classes in school.

To keep an eye on the spending of ratepayers' money, one third of the school's managers would now be appointed by the Education Committee. By 1905 this authority was fixing holidays with the Christmas, Easter and summer breaks adopting what became a long-familiar pattern. Then in 1907 Nuneaton received its Charter of Incorporation as a borough, again including Coton. The overall school name was changed from Chilvers Coton Free School to 'Nuneaton and Chilvers Coton Church of England School'. However, two schools remained, one for boys and one for girls with separate Headteachers. Letterheads now had the local authority name before the school name.

Four new Schools were now built by the Council to ease the pupil overcrowding in the area: Queen's Road 1905, Stockingford 1907, Attleborough 1910 and finally one in Coton parish, Fitton Street, also in 1910. In his history of Nuneaton Ted Veasey remarked on the 'modern' architecture of these schools, 'classrooms round a spacious central hall'. Coton Free school, by contrast, was more old-fashioned and higgledy-piggledy. The opening of these other local schools was expected to ease congestion but it did so only to a limited extent. A major factor in growth was that a higher proportion of children than ever now remained at school until 13 or 14 years of age, aiming for the higher 'Standards' of achievement. Also, absences were declining. At the Girls' school in June 1907 a silver medal was presented to Annie Flowers for five years unbroken attendance, something unlikely 25 years earlier. Some of the improvement in attendance rates had been very recent. In 1900 the figure of 93% was described as 'probably the highest percentage in the history of the school'; and this was maintained. In 1904, 37 came from the Infants' school to the Girls' school though nine were illiterate. However, by the early 20th Century Infant schools were dealing more effectively with the basic literacy and numeracy of standards one and two. Some still left early, labour certificates allowing them to work half the week, if they had reached a minimum standard of attainment, and so attend school part-time. This continued for several years and in 1896-7 there were still eighteen boys and four girls affected. It must have been disrupting not only for their own learning but for their full time colleagues as well.

Evening Classes

Improved attendance and staying longer reflected social change. Some of those who had missed schooling, or forced to leave earlier than they would have wanted, now took advantage of an Evening Continuation class which was active at Coton school in the decade 1893-1903. These classes developed rapidly countrywide after additional funds had been made available by central government in 1892. The subjects proposed were partly elementary: arithmetic, reading and writing, but also more advanced subjects such as physiology – respiration, the skeleton, circulation and digestion. Studies included dissection. A few years later modern history and electricity and magnetism were introduced. One idea was to fill a gap between the ages of 13 – a common leaving age – and 15, when new technical schools, such as Nuneaton's mining school, would be prepared to accept students. The Evening School was financed with a grant from the newly established national body, the Technical Education Committee.

A report of 1897-8 referred to evening classes 'well taught [by the school's teachers] …under efficient discipline and doing useful work'. Commercial history lessons especially were reported as given in an interesting manner. The only criticism was whether the work was too advanced. But it showed the strong desire for self-improvement that spread more widely at the turn of the century. At its peak in 1899 there were 50 girls and 23 boys involved. The girls studied some distinctive subjects: needlework, hygiene, singing and laundry work. The 'wish list' for items to aid the teaching included a sewing machine, glass bottles for experiments, an enema syringe, microscopic sections of specimens, physiological diagrams and Benger's liquor pepticus, a preparation to – in this case at least – help the study of digestion rather than digestion itself. The demand for the Continuation School declined as children who desired it began to stay longer at day school but it had been important for a few years. In very different circumstances it is reminiscent of the children one hundred years before, who attended the Free School when young and afterwards the Sunday school.

Educational Progress and Social Change

Education in Coton was clearly improving: in November 1903 inspectors reported of the Girls' school that there was 'very little to criticise, much to praise'. But the overcrowding prevented the Headmistress from having 'more time for general supervision'. The Girls' school, now led by Kate Wilson, was again commended at this time and there was a growing professionalism: the HMI inspection noted 'enthusiastic workers' and, as for the staff 'they give them a considerable part of their out of school time'. 'Schemes of work are detailed and carefully planned'. As well as supervising the whole school Kate Wilson taught the top class. Pupil teachers – in Coton often later than elsewhere - had begun to replace the old monitors, though in December 1903 the school still advertised for a new monitor. The Boys' school had been similarly praised a few months earlier for 'careful and intelligent instruction'. In 1911 the 'energy and thoughtfulness' of the Headmaster, George Mosedale, was supported by 'efficient staff' encouraging 'self-reliance and individual work'.

Not surprisingly, pupils' standards were rising. This was seen in both theory and practice and assisted by the disappearance in the 1890s of the restrictive Payment by Results system of the Revised Code. No longer did the view prevail so widely that girls and boys of working-class origin should be kept at their original social level and not educated above it. In 1909 local bye-laws ruled that no child could leave school until they were 13 or had attained Standard six. Social mobility began to increase and wider opportunities beckoned with the possibility of secondary education for both boys and girls. Some took advantage of a pupil-teacher scheme developed at Nuneaton Boys' Grammar school (King Edward's). Scholarships to the same school became accessible as the number offered increased markedly with financial aid from the local authority. In August 1906 the news that two boys had achieved these scholarships, Frank Radcliffe and Ralph Mosedale (son of the Headmaster), was celebrated with a half day holiday. More awards were won in subsequent years, three in 1909. Soon afterwards the girls had the opportunity to follow suit. The Nuneaton Girls' High School opened in 1910 and the following year Ida Cave won a scholarship to attend. In April 1914 four girls went to the High School and, like the boys, there was a steady stream thereafter. No longer was the school giving merely straightforward and unambitious elementary education; it now had the additional function of judging ability and potential and identifying possible scholarship candidates, even if, at this stage, it was not expected to be many.

Sport and Physical Training had evolved out of military drill and proved popular. Girls' netball was played on a ground at Heath End and boys' cricket provided considerable success in competition. In July 1909 it was reported that 'this school is again at the head of the Nuneaton Schools' cricket league'. Twenty years later in 1929 Alfred Loveridge played for England schoolboys against Wales in a soccer international. These achievements helped a sense of comradeship and a feeling of belonging to a community that had been less apparent in the more individualistic Victorian age. A very different initiative in this regard was the wearing of a school cap, introduced in September 1925, navy blue and gold. One common lecture from a previous era still made frequent appearances. On 1st September 1925 a talk on the 'evil effects of alcohol' was delivered to all children.

Parental desire for a more advanced education for their children increased noticeably towards the end of the war of 1914-18. The Education Act of 1918 raised the school leaving age to 14 without any exceptions such as half-time working. So, despite the development of other schools, numbers at Coton remained high, well over 350 altogether, with 175 Girls and 186 boys in 1923, rising slightly by the end of the decade (see Appendix Three). Children were staying on

Girls playing outside the school

longer; for instance, 70 boys were now over 12. By the early 1920s 131 children out of 358 had reached Standard five or above, suggesting many of them were capable of higher level work. 70 girls had reached this level but only 61 boys. Local authorities were obliged to ensure that more advanced courses were laid on in elementary schools to cater for 'the older and more intelligent children.'

Buildings and Facilities

These developments found buildings where alterations and expansion had taken place in the previous century in the 1840s, 1870s and 1890s. They had been designed for an earlier age of fewer children and a large class schoolroom mentality that was being increasingly challenged. But, like many other church schools, no more major changes were undertaken. The buildings were now ill-fitting and many of the improvements were wear and tear replacements which could be financed by the Council. For instance in the Girls' school over fifty desks arrived in two stages between 1904 and 1908. There was a little progress in other areas: the Boys' heating was upgraded in 1906 with nine incandescent gas burners. In 1905 Tobin's tubes – upright flues to improve ventilation – were inserted in the large schoolroom. Activities widened: in 1910 girls began to go swimming and the school library developed during the generation where the majority became literate and lacked the later distractions of cinema and radio. Every girl in the top class was required to read at least twelve books with boxes of them borrowed from Nuneaton Library.

Curriculum and Discipline

The curriculum continued to develop and lessons could be quite inventive. In history a facsimile of a death mask of Charles I would have been a star attraction in 1902. In 1899 an Inspector was very taken with the discipline of the boys, in particular the inventive way staff dealt with the awkward geography of the rooms: 'the marching of the children from the large school room to the classroom while singing was certainly striking and showed the most excellent discipline and order'. One or two reached a very high level of performance: in March 1901 twelve year old Clement Clay, a widow's son, received a medal from Lord Strathcona, High Commissioner for Canada, for proficiency in the geography of clouds. Three months later Clay won a scholarship to attend Bablake school.

Girls' and Boys' curriculum would show some differences with for instance needlework for one and handicrafts for the other. In girls' needlework a specialist teacher had been employed as early as 1876. In July 1901 it was, intriguingly, seen as the subject to pursue in hot weather instead of arithmetic. In December 1913 the over elevens in the Boys' school attended a Handicraft Centre. Inspectors frequently noted the 'distinctly good' tone and discipline. The attendance battles at the end of the 19th Century had been largely won and usually over 90% of children were now regularly present.

Empire and World War

The school was not unaffected by the strong imperialistic attitude of the generation immediately prior to the First World War. The half day holiday granted on the news of the relief of Ladysmith (during the Boer War) in March 1900 set a trend. From 1902 there was a half day holiday on 24 May, Empire Day. Special classes were arranged on 'our empire, its growth, extent, population and the duties of its citizens'. In February 1915 boys and girls were taken to see local soldiers start on a united route march. In April 1915 Edmund Manet, a former scholar, explained his role on a mine-sweeper. In June 1915 an old boy, James Knight, a former brickyard labourer who had been wounded at Neuve Chapelle, also spoke. The strongly pro-French flavour of 14 July 1915 would have surprised an earlier generation: on Bastille Day the school held a French flag day and had a specific lesson on France (Britain's war allies), giving money to a French relief fund. A war savings club raised money as part of the National Savings movement inaugurated in 1916. In June 1921 the school War Memorial was unveiled with 67 names, a high number for the size of the institution.

The war affected staffing; male teachers such as Mr. Williams were called up, but there were other effects. At the start of September 1915 Mrs Tite was reported absent helping with the clerical work connected with the National Registration scheme, rapidly recording the occupational details of all men between 15 and 65 not in the armed forces. In May 1917 she was allowed a day off as her husband was on leave for 24 hours before being posted abroad. In November 1915 Thomas Ashby, a P.O.W.,

The memorial to the fallen of World War I

was kept supplied with parcels of goods. Fred Mosedale's wife, Rosellen, worked in the school when he was called up but left in April 1919 after he was demobilised. On 11th November 1919, in answer to the King's appeal, special lessons were held until 10.45a.m. and then the names of the deceased from the Boys' school were read out and a salute taken.

George Mosedale and Florence Towe

One of the reasons for the growing success of the two schools was effective Headteaching. The dominant figure in the Boys' school was George Mosedale, Headmaster over 40 years from 1887 until his retirement in December 1929. He soon made a favourable impression. As early as 9th June 1887 it was reported that 'A considerable improvement has already taken place under the new Master.'

George was born in Portsmouth though he had soon moved to Staffordshire, home of his father's family. As a pupil teacher at Barton-Under-Needwood in 1880 aged 15 he received a first class certificate each year until 1884. George then attended Saltley Training College

An Edwardian classroom: George and Fred Mosedale teaching at the School

from 1884-6 and achieved the Archbishop's Certificate in Divinity (first class) in October 1886. In June 1887 the Diocesan Inspector reported 'very satisfactory progress' in the five months he had been at Coton. In 1890 he obtained a first class in the elementary stage of animal physiology and in 1908 a Licentiate from the College of Preceptors, as opposed to being a mere Associate.

His religious instruction was highly praised. It was always inspected separately on a regular basis by the diocesan clergy. In 1911 the inspector waxed lyrical about the boys in this subject; they were 'a privilege to examine'. The teaching did not produce mechanical understanding, he said, but a real awareness of the application of Christian principles to everyday lives. Like the Newdegates, the direct influence of the Church had declined a little but was still considerable. There were lectures from the Church Missionary Society and Chilvers Coton vicars Dodds and (from 1928) Davies were frequent visitors. An examination of the 1662 Prayer Book in 1927 coincided with the debate in Parliament on the advisability of a new one. One diocesan inspector remarked that the children had found some of its language hard to understand.

George Mosedale was an outstanding Headmaster. Towards the end of his career inspectors reviewed his achievements in the Boys' school. 'By his earnest and close attention to the welfare of successive generations of pupils, he has earned their respect and gratitude', high praise for an official report. Another commented that he had 'stamped his personality upon the place' and had 'a fine record of service'. George Clarke attended the school between 1896 and 1898 and described George Mosedale and his younger brother (by 13 years) and fellow teacher Fred Mosedale as 'good sound men, real practical teachers' who 'kept the boys up to their work without any bullying and dealt with any unruliness firmly, but without harshness'. Teacher George was impressed with scholar George and the Headmaster was disappointed when the young man left at 13 and a half: he had hoped he would become a pupil teacher. But promising scholars leaving at this age were still all too common before the 1920s and even later.

Under Mosedale and the Heads of the Girls' school - Ellen Mottram 1888-1897, Kate Wilson 1897-1911 and Florence Towe 1911-1932, Coton's education was transformed. They were now in charge of a range of staff, running a larger school with some separate classrooms, moving away from the old concept of one large schoolroom, though the survival of these large rooms affected the architectural make up of the buildings. But Headmaster and Headmistress still operated in a size of school small enough for them to be known by all pupils.

Like Mosedale, Kate Wilson, Headmistress 1897-1911, guided the Girls' school through the time of major growth, an increase in staff, local authority involvement and an ever-widening curriculum. Her successor Florence Towe continued this tradition. Unlike most of the previous head teachers of Coton, Florence was born and bred in the parish in 1882, the third child of five with her father James a master tailor and mother Elizabeth a worsted weaver, living in Coton

Road where a family tailoring business developed. Florence attended the Coton Free School and in 1899 became a pupil teacher until 1902. She returned to the school in 1903 to teach there for a further year. Becoming a certificated teacher, she took a post in Alum Rock from 1905 to 1910 and then taught briefly at Vicarage Street School Nuneaton before assuming the headship of the Girls' school at Coton. A school pupil from the 1920s, Kath Smith, describes Florence Towe as an impressive figure, well-dressed with a 'strong voice' but with a sympathetic 'motherly' approach and someone who used the cane but sparingly. Kath recalls Florence as very much part of Coton life, seeing the children frequently when she went shopping or to church and sometimes giving them apples from her garden. In 1925 inspectors praised the Girls' school, remarking on 'many attractive elements in the curriculum'. The inspectors added that it was obvious that girls enjoyed their school life and were ready to take an active part in lessons that appealed to them.' This did not include all subjects. In some 'the girls appear to have little mastery over much of the material.' Algebra proved difficult for some.

Progress Made

By the 1920s both schools had the reputation of efficient well-run institutions despite buildings which restricted developments rather than encouraged them. Understanding of pupils' needs increased: in 1917 special lessons were given to Standard 3 boys considered backward. As older able pupils' stayed on, teachers needed to reach a high standard themselves in an increasingly wide range of subjects. Their growing professionalization was becoming apparent. By 1921 there was 'specialist teaching' in history and geography as well as singing, gardening, cookery and woodwork, the last two sometimes at the Educational Centre in Coton Road. The children would be examined at the end of each year. Inspectors reported on 'a wide and varied range of study' where 'the teaching of history is wisely not confined to Britain.' Children were staying on longer at school and generally getting employment when they left. In 1928 there were 21 leavers from the Boys' school: 17 were for employment, two moved away and two went on scholarships to the Grammar school. This was typical for that decade. But at a school such as Coton they did not have the facilities to study science. The traditional pen and inkwell remained.

Days off for local events were gradually being replaced by outings further afield, a popular and effective way of widening horizons. One such was the British Empire Wembley Exhibition of 1925. There was also a visit to the Houses of Parliament (1928) where pupils marvelled over escalators and underground trains and, for some, their first ever trip on a train. In 1929 an outing to Liverpool involved 'shopping' and a visit to the Cathedral. Whipsnade Zoo was visited by the girls in 1930. Periodic talks on the League of Nations starting in 1925 reflected the different attitude to world affairs from pre-war imperialistic bluster. Nature study proved popular with many girls with trips to local bluebell woods. In 1924 five girls kept a nature study diary throughout the year. Nor was the great local literary hero neglected. There were trips to Astley and Griff House to see where she was brought up but the main celebration was in 1919 on the centenary of George Eliot's birth. In 1927 there was a presentation of a scene from Mill on the Floss - 'Miss Pullett tries on her new bonnet'. acted by Mabel Chandler, May Muscutt and Ethel Taylor in St George's Hall with music provided by 'Standard Seven' (i.e. more advanced) pupils.

Despite some privations caused by industrial conflict, pupils were generally fitter than hitherto. Since 1905 there had been health visitors and from 1908 medical examinations. But of course illness was reduced not eradicated. There were still a few cases of scabies, scarlet fever and diphtheria. In April 1913 eight boys were excluded for ringworm and in March 1915 twelve girls. A serious flu epidemic coincided with the end of the First World War in 1918. On the 25th October it was reported that the schools were 'greatly affected' by flu. They planned to close for two weeks until November 18th but were not finally opened until the beginning of December. Children's heads continued to be examined regularly and occasionally someone was sent home. By 1920 a dentist visited and more preventative work was gradually being undertaken. Improvements in the 1920s were noticeable though two girls contracted smallpox in 1924 and there was another flu epidemic in 1926. Occasionally logbooks reported the death of a child. Nor were teachers immune, one getting scarlet fever in 1921. In September 1930 Albert Ernest Hoddell died aged 50 and the school was closed for his funeral with wreaths from staff and pupils. Formerly a teacher in Derbyshire he had been at the school since 1907 and coached the cricket team. (Perhaps this accounts for his son Tom's reputation as a good local cricketer). His daughter Iris, born in 1907, also taught at the school in the 1920s before moving to Queen's Road School in 1931.

One visible sign of the transformation of the schools was in staffing. Long gone were the days of just one Schoolmaster or Schoolmistress with perhaps one inexperienced assistant. By the 1920s the Boys' and Girls' schools both had five full time staff though not all were able to have separate classrooms. Individual teachers would focus on a particular class most of the time, concentrating on their pupils achieving one of the Standards, though some subjects could be taught by a specialist. Whereas, since 1846, most teachers had come up by the pupil teacher route from an early age, learning the craft by experience, now the younger staff generally came from a variety of Training Colleges, and were more formally qualified than in previous generations. At first there was an all-male staff in the Boys' school and an all-female one in the Girls' school but the association of female teachers with younger children was growing, starting with the Infant School. In 1904, 22 year old Lucy Harris from Atherstone was appointed to the Boys' school as the first female teacher. However, women were still expected to leave upon marriage such as Miss Wright in 1926. There was a minor exception: when 'no satisfactory appointment' could be made to replace her in December 1929, Miss Greenham, about to be married, was allowed to stay for the time being. She was replaced the following February.

All this was undertaken against the background of continued overcrowding where problems continued. A report of 1922 referred to 'structural defects' which put a strain on both teachers and pupils. There was not enough space. Four classes worked side by side in a large room with only a low movable screen in the centre. The following year one boy was slightly injured when a slate fell from the roof. Perhaps the development of open-air teaching in hot summer weather in this period was not merely following the fresh-air philosophy of the time but giving more space inside for the remaining pupils. Yet despite the problems the boys worked 'with steady diligence'. In 1930 the atmosphere of the Girls' school was praised since 'the interest and enthusiasm of the Headmistress and her staff go far to counteract the depressing working conditions'. There had been a little improvement in 1927 when electric light replaced gas. The nature of the building made expansion difficult and awkward. The large fire in the main Girls' schoolroom was insufficient to heat the adjacent classrooms and Kath Smith recalls that overcoats could be worn in very cold weather. Class sizes, though smaller than in the 19th Century, were still large and, between the wars, forty was a common number. After the government expenditure cuts of 1922 many classes were expected for a time to have fifty on their books.

On occasions one could be reminded of the many days for time off for non-health reasons, common in a previous era. In October 1928 poor attendance was noted as a result of boys going potato picking.

Nor had poverty disappeared. In 1924, twenty two pairs of boots were distributed to needy children, through the trustees of the late Harry Fieldhouse, the editor of Nuneaton's first daily newspaper the Midland Daily Tribune, who died at the age of 56 after being knocked down by a motor bike. The continuing importance of mining to the district was emphasised in 1926: free breakfast was offered to children suffering because of the coal dispute: on the first day five came; by June 3rd there were 43. School kept going: the children's difficulties were caused by domestic privation rather than lack of education. A local butcher presented two flanks of beef to the school to be distributed among the children of miners who were on strike for much longer than the nine days of the General Strike in May. Rural traditions were not forgotten. In 1922 there was a day off for the County Agricultural show in Caldwell Park. A reminder of past priorities was a half day holiday to celebrate Sir Francis and Lady Newdegate's ruby wedding in 1928.

The End of Two Separate Schools

In December 1929 George Mosedale retired at the age of 64 having been Head since January 1887, almost 43 years. Other major changes were afoot. After the Hadow Report of 1926 there were hopes that the school leaving age would be raised to 15. Educational policy favoured a clear break at eleven years of age and then a minimum of at least three or possibly four years in another school. This would now happen in Coton. A school was being constructed on an adjacent site to Coton Free School, to be called Swinnerton School after the distinguished

Robert Swinnerton

local alderman and educational philanthropist. Coton would become a junior mixed school teaching 7-11 year olds and older pupils would pass on to Swinnerton. As well as following national policy it was hoped this would ease overcrowding. The new head of the Boys' school, Albert Edward Ascott, succeeded Mosedale in January 1930 and in April the two separate schools were given a formal letter of closure by the County Council. Ascott was destined to be the Head of the new combined school which was to be given the name 'Chilvers Coton Junior Mixed School' (see Appendix One). Not in the best of health, Florence Towe retired as Headmistress at just 50 (she died in 1937). On 23rd March 1932 the two schools were combined. The school's final era was about to begin: it did not prove a quiet finale.

Avenue Road during the 1930s

Chapter Four:
Amalgamation, Bombings And Closure
The Last Years Of The School: The Building Survives

How do you think you would write or speak about anything more difficult if you knew no more of grammar than he does? [**Middlemarch**]

The school's final years were not uneventful. There was the challenge of a growing local population, the financial strains of a partly church-run school and the reforms in state education leading to the end of all-through 7-14 schools. As if this were not enough, Nazi bombs produced an even severer kind of pressure.

The effects of change on the new school: 1932-40
1932 was not the easiest of times to begin a new educational venture with national depression, cuts in schools' budgets and reductions in teachers' salaries; elementary teachers at schools like Coton were the

Hill Top Estate

lowest paid to start with. The new combined school for seven-eleven years began with just 209 boys and girls. In August 1933, seventy six over 11s left to attend Swinnerton school. But would this produce a less crowded building? Not for long. The new Council estate being constructed at nearby Hill Top would soon provide additional pupils. Ten from there were admitted as the school began. Within a month total numbers were up to 231 and the average class size to 38.5. By February 1933 as more 'Hill Toppers' arrived, numbers had again gone up to 266 and further increases occurred before 1939. In 1935 there were eight classes with eight teachers – plus a headmaster who, unlike before, could concentrate on the general running of the school or filling in for absentees. By 1937 new classes had been created to try to absorb the increased numbers without further disruption. But in 1938 children due to go 'up' to secondary school were retained as Swinnerton was full.

By this time Sir Francis Newdegate had died in January 1936. He had seen the school transformed in many ways, not least in the reduction of his own family's role. The Head attended the funeral but unlike Charles Newdegate's death in 1887, the school did not close for the day. The Newdegate link now reduced further. The school was completely taken over by the local authority who would appoint all teachers except anybody reserved for denominational religious instruction. It was re-named, with a strange combination of looking back and looking forward, 'Shepperton (Temporary) Council School'. In January 1939 there were 274 pupils but from now on the future of the school was in doubt.

The buildings required extensive capital expenditure. In the bad weather of January 1939 snow entered through the windows and school was delayed while the valiant caretaker undertook a major mopping-up operation. The following winter was equally cold and an official complaint was made to the education authorities about conditions. A series of low inside temperatures was recorded but none surpassed that of Room 6 at 8.45 on the morning of the 22nd January 1940:

The Wem Brook, approximately 300 yards from Coton Free School

29 degrees Fahrenheit (-1.5°C). Some work was carried out in the Easter holiday of 1940 when Nuneaton Gas Company installed a new heating system of 19 radiators. But events soon overtook the chance of further improvements.

The Curriculum

The school continued to be praised by inspectors. Albert Ascott had re-organised the timetable and curriculum and in 1936 inspectors commented upon a 'carefully planned scheme' delivered by 'conscientious' teachers to 'well-mannered' pupils. Arithmetic was seen as the best subject, writing somewhat weaker. Once again the building bore the brunt of criticism with the lack of a central hall 'a severe handicap'. The rooms that could have served this purpose had to be used as classrooms, divided into two.

Games developed, encouraged particularly by new teacher Ted Grubb, (appointed 1932) whose previous sporting prowess at Nuneaton Grammar school would have been well known. Cricket and football practices now became common, to attain the highest possible standard. During the 1930s new technology began to affect presentation of lessons. In January 1934 three members of staff attended a lecture on school broadcasting in the local St. George's Hall. For those of a more musical turn 28 boys and girls took part in a concert organised by the Nuneaton Elementary Schools' Musical Association. But facilities were hardly high-tech. In September 1936 a second-hand gramophone with 14 records was presented by the Education Committee. In September 1942 a wireless receiver was obtained and broadcast lessons listened to. They included talks on health by the radio doctor and music and movement – appropriate subjects for those suffering from the cold.

There had developed an increasing belief in the utility of intelligence tests to assess the achievements and potential of all pupils. It was believed that these would help to determine which children would be suitable for a more academic secondary education. February 1935 saw a 45 minute IQ test for these special places –a forerunner of the 11+ examination that would take place after 1945, by which time all pupils were to attend a secondary school of some form or other. In March 1935 the school held a ten-minute practice test before the official test, instructed by the County's Director of Education. A gradual increase in the numbers going on to secondary education helped to drive these developments. Special places replaced scholarships, a sign of greater numbers being selected. But demand outstripped supply and many secondary school places still had to be paid for, outside the resources of many of the school's parents. National educational cuts in the early 1930s delayed the trend to secondary education for all, especially in a school such as Coton with its distinctive social profile.

Social Aspects

The majority of the school's pupils still came, as they always had done, from the working class. Miners' sons and daughters still attended but, increasingly since the 1860s, the children of ribbon weavers had been replaced by the offspring of labourers in the brickyards, textile operatives and railway workers. The strong charitable traditions of the school took on a different turn in the 1930s. In the past these had usually been based on local initiative. Now it was national. Concerns about poor diets for many children led to the free distribution of milk to needy schoolchildren and, on 9th October 1934, 170 bottles were given out in the school. As to the physical safety of children the emphasis had changed to a greater awareness of the dangers of traffic accidents, particularly prevalent in the 1930s. Work on road safety one day was followed by a visit to the Ritz Cinema the next to see the film Better Safe than Sorry. After 1945 school meals developed and, initially, 65 were served dinner, 19 receiving them free. In view of the large numbers of old boys who were wartime casualties it was not surprising that the 11th November was always marked as a special day. In 1935 for instance chrysanthemums bought by the children were laid on the War Memorial.

The pupils moving to Swinnerton school usually stayed until 14, and then left, many without paper qualifications, still low on the ladder of formal educational achievement. There was general acceptance by the 1930s that, for children from a school like Coton to get the most out of their education, it would require the abolition of all fees in secondary schools, not merely the granting of a few scholarship places. The view that working-class children – with a few outstanding exceptions – could not benefit from more advanced education was increasingly questioned. But cuts in all schools' budgets in both the early 1920s and early 1930s delayed both the further raising of the school leaving age and the increased funding of secondary education. The ending of fees in these schools was only achieved after 1944.

The Staff

The Headmaster of the new combined school, Albert Ascott, hailed from Bath where he had been a pupil teacher. Born in 1897 he had been wounded in the army in 1915 before attending St Paul's, Cheltenham, Training College. Thereafter he had taught in Coleshill. Keen on swimming, he encouraged sports, organised the combining of the two separate schools and maintained the standards of his predecessors. There were eight assistant staff, four male and four female. To a modern mind this seems an excellent balance but not to an Inspector in 1933. He criticised the school for having 50% male teachers in a junior school as 'not a suitable proportion' complaining that 'girls of seven are taught by a man.' Two new teachers joined the existing staff. From the Boys' school there were Miss Harris, formerly the only female teacher there, the long serving Fred Mosedale and W.H. Crabtree, the latter staying until moving next door to Swinnerton in 1938. From the Girls' school came Miss Milburn and Mrs. Ford. It was still hard for female teachers to remain when they married. A partial dispensation for Miss Milburn was made in December 1935. She was given permission to stay until the following July. Only two teachers were now uncertificated. Six were responsible for a different 'Standard' in the school. There was a steady turnover in the coming years, particularly in wartime, but Headmaster Ascott remained.

Fred Mosedale reached the age of 65 in January 1944 and was allowed to stay on a further 18 months, seeing out the war before he retired. He had begun as a pupil teacher aged 14 in 1891 and so served 54 years. Since retirements and pensions developed in the late 19th Century he must have been one of the longest serving teachers at the same school in the country let alone the county. Remembered by Kath Smith as having golden hair and thin horn-rimmed glasses, Fred Mosedale had seen many changes. One wonders what he made of a teachers' conference attended by the Coton staff in March 1944 on sex education.

His retirement was marked by a special presentation of £16 10s (£16.50) and a tobacco pouch with a further ten shilling note inside. This event was attended by the Mayor and Mayoress of Nuneaton, the Chairman of the Education Committee and former Head George Mosedale, his elder brother, now over 80.

The Buildings

The buildings were described as having 'many defects'. On the west side there was insufficient light because trees and wooden fences were in a dangerous state of repair. Lighting, heating and ventilation all required attention. There was brief drama on the 6th December 1933 when fire broke out. A heater had set a towel alight at 3pm but it was extinguished without serious damage. Until the late 1930s the Newdegates were still responsible for buildings: 'I have written to Mr. Whitfield, agent for Arbury pointing out the urgent need for repairs to the Lavatory wall' explained the Headmaster in July 1936. But with major capital investment needed there seemed little likelihood of immediate improvement. The Education Act of 1936 promised building grants to Voluntary non-provided schools like Coton, partly to deal with the implications of a further raising of the school leaving age. But war was to intervene.

The War

The most dramatic period in the history of Coton School came at the end of the 1930s. Awareness of the dangerous international diplomatic situation became apparent to all children when on 20th September 1938 prayers in assembly were for peace, particularly for the 'Czechoslovak problem'. A week later there were more prayers 'in view of the possibility of an outbreak of war'. The following day children were taught how to make use of a civilian respirator. Within a couple of days news of the Munich settlement ended the practice with gas masks almost before they had begun, but Munich merely postponed war for a year.

The outbreak of fighting at the start of September 1939 coincided with the start of a new school year which was postponed for nearly two weeks until the 18th. Pupils discovered they would soon be practising marching into trenches. The Headmaster attended instruction in fire fighting and the rest of the staff first aid lectures. The timings of the school day were altered: 8.45 to 11.45am and 1.pm to just 3.05 pm so that the school could be cleaned before the blackout. After the lull of the phoney war over the winter of 1939-40 the first three air-raid warnings occurred on 3rd April 1940. By June four trenches at the adjacent Swinnerton School were ready for Coton's use, though the approach to them was initially considered rough and dangerous and they were later levelled. Male staff were always likely to be called up – Mr. Payne went for an examination for military service in September 1940 and Mr. Burrows enlisted in the RAF in the following month. Throughout 1940 there were continuous air raid warnings. As with the First World War money was raised through war savings, amounting to £37 by November 1940.

At this stage Coventry was suffering more directly from war than Nuneaton. On 18th November 1940, three days after the Coventry blitz, Coton school was closed for a day so that teachers could do a billeting survey for the reception of Coventry evacuees. A few days later nine of these were admitted to the school. Conservation assumed the kind of high profile that, after the war, had to wait a further forty years before the spirit of re-cycling re-asserted itself on an equivalent scale. Scrap iron collections began in the summer of 1940. There were frequent air-raid warnings which disrupted the smooth routines of the school.

Lessons and normal school life continued as far as possible, not only for Coton children, but also for the evacuees. Some of these had come from London and would, in March 1941, take their London County

Wartime damage of Chilvers Coton Church, opposite the school

Council Special Place examination. But these evacuees had not come to a place immune from attack. On 17th May 1941 a high explosive bomb fell on the south side of the church of All Saints Chilvers Coton opposite the school. The church was wrecked save for the tower and the school badly damaged. Roofs, doors, windows, ceilings and partition screens were all affected. With serious disruption elsewhere in the area the decision was taken on 19th May to close all local schools for the moment. For the next few days staff spent school hours clearing debris and the following week volunteered to assist at a communal feeding station at Manor Park School. At the same time Headmaster Ascott assisted with 'first aid' repairs at the Infants' School. In the middle of June the children returned to their studies but had to attend half-time at Swinnerton School. Coton, with greater damage, would be closed for longer. Clearly conditions were cramped at Swinnerton and so different classes of children attended at different times of the day. Attendance was quite high though it emerged that about 20 children had left the district in the midst of the troubles. In that year's summer holiday children could still come in for their free milk; meals were provided, a custom which would continue after the war.

It would be some time before some normality returned. The Coton School building was re-opened on 17th November 1941 with hours from 9.50 to 12.30 and 2-4. Some lessons were held in Coton Parish Hall. With further air raids, frequent news of fatalities, a bombed school and town and a cold winter, life was tough. So a pleasant diversion occurred when at the darkest time of the war on 25th February 1942 King George VI and Queen Elizabeth visited Nuneaton officially to inspect the Civil Defence forces but also to try to boost the morale of a badly affected area. The Coton schoolchildren lined the Coton Road to watch the Royal couple. Air raids continued: on 26th May 1942 there was a serious attack in the early hours. Only 70% attended school in the morning but 99% returned in the afternoon. Things to smile about were the occasional successes of pupils in gaining scholarships to local Grammar Schools. Even in the worst times this did not disappear. In 1942 Edward A. Veasey was among the successes, going on to King Edward VI School and a distinguished career in history teaching and local historical research in which he also inspired many others.

Former pupil Ted Veasey

The school looked for ways to contribute to the war effort. This produced a revival of an old custom: to aid the dig for victory some children went potato picking at Burton Hastings and Copston Magna in early October 1942. Exactly a year later, as the balance of power in the war began to shift with an intense bombing campaign of Germany, the schools took part in a day of national prayer. Staff and pupils worked through the October half term in order to make up for the lost hours. The school was still in a mess with only temporary repairs. However, in the summer of 1944 new ceilings and fresh plastering produced more substantial improvement. The start of the autumn term that year was delayed for a time, while the changes were completed. But conditions were still poor – there was no major re-decoration.

The end of the war in Europe in early May 1945 provided a cause for celebration. The school log book records that on 10th May there was 'poor attendance, owing to the atmosphere of general rejoicing'. At a special assembly a few days later the headmaster reminded boys and girls 'what we had been saved from' and how other lands had now been liberated from Nazi occupation. Later in the year came another special holiday to mark victory over Japan and the end of the World War.

Post-War

The days of the school were now numbered, although damage that required re-decoration was undertaken in September 1946. Despite heating improvements, the winter of 1947 proved tough with low attendances and electricity cuts between 9am and 12noon and 2pm and 4pm. No outdoor playtime was possible for several weeks. Numbers continued to be high with 368 scholars in 1951.

All schools emerged from the war faced with a changed educational landscape. The 1944 Education Act ensured that all pupils would be entitled to both primary and secondary education and the school leaving age was finally raised to 15 in 1947. Pupils from Coton would take an eleven plus examination, after which they would pass on to one of the town's three Grammar Schools or attend others schools, now reconstructed as Secondary Moderns. In September 1946 the last of the younger leavers departed, 49 transferring to the new Secondary Moderns and just six to Grammar schools. The proportions reflected both the relatively low number of Grammar school places in war-torn Nuneaton and the comparative social deprivation of the Coton School intake.

Greater attention was now paid to children struggling to keep up and Mr. Pantin specialised in this work. There was a steady turnover of staff in those last years, a combination of uncertainty over the future and the poor facilities they had to cope with. Improvements were slow: forty new desks came in 1951 but new chairs were urgently needed. The new Middlemarch school opened nearby in 1952 just in time to take the additional children in the 7-11 age range as a result of the post-war birth rate bulge and so the long-term plan to close the school finally matured. 23rd June 1954 was its last day with most children and staff moving to Caldwell County Junior School.

The End...
But not the End
Coton Free School had ended but the building was still standing. It was not expected to survive in the long run but for the moment it was still useful. At first it served as an annexe to the adjacent Swinnerton School and also as an overspill building for the nearby St Joseph's Roman Catholic School. But with the expectation of closure and probable demolition, no improvements were made to a building already seen as cramped and old-fashioned. In 1967, when still being used, Nuneaton M.P. Leslie Huckfield referred to it as 'one of the worst buildings one could expect to come across in primary education'.

In 1973 the comprehensive re-organisation in the area meant schooling in Coton Free School finally ended. It was taken over by the Parks Department as a convenient building to store heavy machinery used on the nearby Pingles fields. Inevitably, the building deteriorated in this period and in June 1987 it was reported that the Council had approved demolition plans and that it could be pulled down within three months on the grounds that it was of little architectural merit.

But this announcement produced immediate opposition and another eventful period in the building's varied history. John Burton of the Bedworth Society argued that there were too few examples of its kind in the area and it could not afford to be lost. The point was a more profound one than one of mere architectural connoisseurship. The School was neither beautiful nor, though distinctive, exceptionally unusual in appearance; its value lay in its historical role: a school for the people and thus a living reminder to the ordinary folk of Chilvers Coton and Nuneaton of how they had travelled to where they were. When there were so few other examples of this, the argument went, even to consider pulling it down showed little understanding of the relationship between the town's people and its past. Events moved swiftly. On June 29th a Nuneaton Civic Society was formed as a result of a public meeting with ex-Alderman Smith School teacher Beryl Kerby elected to chair the organisation. Beryl pointed out there were many other old buildings in the Borough worth fighting for. But Coton Free School had been the trigger.

The strong, even intimate, connections of George Eliot to the immediate area gave fuel to the campaign to save the building. The George Eliot Fellowship lent its support and 16 literary societies throughout Britain became involved in opposing demolition including those concerned with Dickens, the Brontës, Kipling and Hardy. Playing the George Eliot card proved an effective move. With strong contributions from figures such as John Burton and Beryl Kerby and also Kathleen Adams of the George Eliot Fellowship, the protest was successful. There were other key people at this time working behind the scenes to change the Council's decision. Notable among them was Rob Hayward, the Conservation Officer for the Council, and Don Jacques, a forthright opposition Councillor who also taught at the school in the 1950s. In August 1987 the Council announced a reprieve. What also aided the outcome was that it was a constructive protest. The proposal was to convert the building into a Heritage Centre for the Nuneaton and Chilvers Coton area. It was a bold conception. The building was described as being in a 'deplorable state inside'. So those wishing to keep the building would have to work hard to achieve some re-construction. However, John Burton had argued at the June 29th meeting that 'I am sure we could find the money to renovate it from somewhere'. This indeed proved to be the case.

But renovation was only the first step. In the frenzied discussion that immediately followed the announcement of the proposed demolition, one Council member remarked that 'I hope the people who want a heritage centre there will be just as keen to run one themselves.' This second challenge was also met. While the Council would retain ownership of the building, a peppercorn rent would be paid and the people of the area – many of them descendants of the school's pupils – would run the Heritage Centre. Beryl Kerby, who was in overall

Beryl Kerby

charge, could claim her second cousin Isabella Streather as a teacher at the school between 1901 and 1907. Responsibility for the building was assumed in 1988.

The Development of the Heritage Centre

Beryl was not without valuable assistance. A Coton Trust was set up to administer the running of the building, with, generally, eight to ten Trustees, including a Secretary and Treasurer, as well as Beryl chairing the organisation. The Centre became a company limited by guarantee, (where members are guarantors rather than shareholders), and was granted charitable status. The brief had been to restore the building and maintain it as a Heritage and Community Centre. It has been amply fulfilled. To make this former school suitable for its new purpose, especially after recent years of relative neglect, there was hard work to be done on guttering, central heating and re-configuring several rooms. New floorboards were laid for the first time since 1884. The Trust had enormous moral and financial support in those early years from Peter Deeley, who was also one of the first Trustees. Beryl Kerby and the Trust were also given invaluable advice and support by both Ella Jepson, who was in practice as an architect in the town throughout her career and Rob Hayward who continued his invaluable assistance by becoming a Trustee. In the 1990s, the Trust had huge practical support from a local teacher and Councillor, Mike Palladino. Extensive decorating of several high-ceilinged rooms was one of several labours of love which called on the skills, persistence and financial assistance of local people. They helped to develop a sense of comradeship and shared purpose among the volunteers which has strengthened and deepened over the years. Now there is a Friends of Chilvers Coton organisation which brings a little more regular income.

Once one of the schoolrooms had been renovated it was possible to think about getting the public into the Centre. They would enter to a distinctly educational atmosphere. Walls were emblazoned with local old school photographs and lists of early 20th Century names of pupils in local elementary schools – not just Coton Free School – who had achieved scholarships and/or county awards of some description.

This remains a visual reminder of the progress of schools like Coton at that period of its history: sending girls and boys to local Grammar schools in a way the 19th Century, with its rigid social hierarchy, did not allow. On the other hand it also serves to show that in this era, before 1944, children of working class origin had frequently to be seen as 'exceptional' students in order to get the educational opportunities of which so many more could have taken advantage.

After continued hard work the Centre started to receive visitors in 1990. An early development was the establishment of one of the classrooms as a Victorian schoolroom which has proved a popular venue for visits over the years, not least from local schoolchildren. Desks were acquired from numerous sources and, given the nature of the building and more committed volunteering, an effective 19th Century atmosphere was created. The Centre took advantage of the Borough's Victorian theme for their Christmas lights opening in 1990 when, on this occasion, money was found for professional actors to re-enact the 19th Century school experience. Visits from local schoolchildren have been a regular feature of the last twenty-five years with 'Victorian' school teachers in attendance. Although most visitors are from the locality the Centre has attracted attention from much further afield, even guests from America and Australia.

Money-raising has been an ever-present theme in the development of the Centre. As National Lottery funding developed in the 1990s vital funds were acquired from Awards for All to assist with interior repairs and refurbishment. There was a grant from WREN towards renewing the roofs at either end of the building, obtained largely through the efforts of Janet Stubbs. There was also a significant grant from BSN (Building Sustainable Neighbourhoods) to assist with secondary glazing. Groups using the building, such as morris men and the model engineers, brought in useful cash and emphasised its role as a building

The Parlour in the present day centre

for community activities. Another early use was for craft fairs and the Centre has played a role in important local events such as the Festival of Arts and Britain in Bloom. The building was therefore certainly not isolated from the rest of the community and the development of the Chilvers Coton Craft Centre units adjacent to the school emphasised this in a physical sense from 1993.

The Centre was developing a room configuration that is still recognisable today with offices, toilets (enlarged and renewed by a donation from Don Jacques when he was Mayor of the Borough in 1995), meeting room, schoolroom and exhibition room. Some of these were named after those linked to the building such as the Mosedale Room – after the former Coton Free School Headmaster – and now containing the computers that he would surely have used had the technology been invented in his day. There is a Newdegate Gallery, and a Streather Room named after Beryl Kerby's father, also a local Headmaster. More recently the schoolroom has been re-named the Beryl Kerby Schoolroom, in honour of the person who did so much to make the venture possible and who oversaw the early successful developments of the Centre. Another room is to be named Millie Barton's Parlour, recognising the references in George Eliot's Amos Barton to the Shepperton (Coton) area and in particular the fictional visits of the caring Free School mistress to the dying Milly.

The George Eliot Fellowship have become just one more of the many organisations using the Centre, the number increasing as time has progressed. Other organisations vary from the local Gurkha veterans and Nepalese residents, the Nuneaton Civic Society, Weightwatchers, a Carers organisation, Diabetic support group, Nuneaton Writers' Circle and the Nuneaton and North Warwickshire Family History Society. The Trust itself organises social and fund-raising events such as quizzes, musical evenings, lectures and slide shows.

At the start of the second decade of the 21st Century some generous bequests and further success with grant applications also made further substantial improvement possible and a widening of

Memorial to Lady Elizabeth

the various roles the building could play from wedding receptions to funeral wakes. In 2011 the largest grant yet obtained - £49,500 - was given by WREN (Waste Recycling Environmental Limited) a provider of money for heritage projects. But grants such as this had to be matched by equivalent cash from the local community. It was forthcoming: with the help of some of the earlier £20,000 donation from Beazer Homes, funds were raised to enable a thorough re-roofing of the central halls at a total cost of just over £60,000. The rest of the Beazer Homes money was added to a donation of £5,000 from the Mayor, Councillor Tom Wilson, to provide a new kitchen at a cost of £8,000. The stripping of the roof timbers from the 1840s revealed the carving of Charles Newdegate's initials, CNN 1844, an uncommonly clear visual illustration of the close relationship of one man with one school for over 50 years.

Charles Newdegate's initials carved in the roof timbers

So now under the energetic and very capable leadership of John Burton the Heritage Centre goes from strength to strength. It is open all day Tuesday as well as Thursday and Saturday mornings with a dedicated and good-natured staff. A small but already well-resourced library/research room has recently been developed and so the Centre will, appropriately, enable local people to investigate the history of the local area. The building has increasingly returned to the original educational intention of those who set up and developed it: to help the local community acquire the knowledge and understanding of their surroundings – and beyond. Long may it continue.

The Centre today

Appendices

Appendix One:
School Name

Chilvers Coton Free School	1735-1907
Nuneaton and Chilvers Coton Church of England School	1907-1932
Chilvers Coton Junior Mixed School	1932-1940
Shepperton (Temporary) Council School.	1940-1953

———◆◆◆———

Appendix Two:
Names of Head Teachers
Dates in bold are *merely probable.*

1697-1733	John Viall, vicar of parish, paid by the Newdigates, possibly for teaching. [1704 Henry Simes mentioned as teacher - possibly assistant to Viall.]	

18th Century School

1736 - 1738	Possibly the curate	Thomas Parker
1743 (or earlier) - 1768 (or later)		Ezra Evisson

Girls' school from mid C19th

Before 1840 - 1848	Ann Morris
1849 - 1874	Sarah Clarke
1875 (early) - 1876 (Dec)	Susannah Nicholas
1877(Jan) - 1888	Sarah Gee
1888 - 1897	Ellen Mottram
1897 - 1911	Kate Wilson
1911 - 32	Florence Towe

Boys' school from mid C19th

? - **1841**	Thomas Clifford
1841 - 1844	John Auld
1844 - 1870	John Clarke
1870 - 1888	Thomas Robinson
1888-1929	George Henry Mosedale
1929-1932	Albert Edward Ascott

Combined school after 1932

1932-1954	Albert Edward Ascott

Appendix Three:
Numbers of children at the school

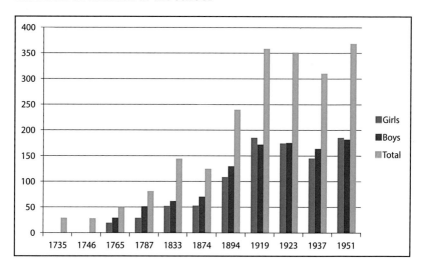

Appendix Four:
Draft of deed for settling a school at Chilvers Coton
by Sir Roger Newdigate 1765

Dame Elizabeth Newdigate widow deceased, late mother of Roger Newdigate formerly purchased a messuage with the appurtenances in Chilvers Coton the which she re-built and converted into a school for the educating of 30 poor children of the said parish which has continued to this time for the same use —and whereas the said Roger Newdigate is willing and desirous to confirm the said charities to augment the same by the annuity by him hereinafter given...

Appendix Five:
Chilvers Coton Sunday School Committee 1787
Sir Roger Newdigate, Bernard Gilpin Ebdall, Thomas Hutchings, Thomas Worthington, William Hill, Mr. Evans, John Clarke, Richard Sketchley, George Taylor.
Masters to be Thomas Buswell and Thomas Spencer

Subscribers:
Sir Roger and Lady Newdigate, Mrs. Beighton, Rev. G. Ebdell, Mr Harper, Thomas Hutchings, William Hill, James Morris, James Pimlott, William Waddams, John Adcock, Thomas Worthington, George Taylor junior, John Clarke, Thomas Moreton, Francis Kinder, Richard Sketchley, John Phillip, John Blyth, Dan Whancock, Thomas Oliver, Rob Smith, John Hawes, Thomas Knight, John Cox, Joseph Dagley, James Scott senior, Francis Ward, Sam Atherstone, William Richardson.

Appendix Six:
A Naughty Boy
On the morning of 20 April 1896 one William Washbourne, a Coton pupil, stole 5/6d (66p) from his mother. Truanting from school he was found late at night by a teacher and taken home. It emerged that he had had quite a day. The money he had spent was all accounted for as follows:
Rail, Nuneaton to Coventry 12d, Coventry to Nuneaton 12d. Biscuits 2d, oranges 2d, ginger ale 1d, pork pie 4d, rail to Tamworth and back 13d, stamps 7d, pork pie at Tamworth 1d, chocolate 2d, show 2d, coffee 1d, chewing gum 1d, tea 2d, fried fish 2d, theatre 6d, sandwiches 2d. Clearly he had 6d in his pocket before he went. The school took action: he was caned and, appropriately one might think, kept in at dinner time without dinner.

Appendix Seven:
Subscription book for Chilvers Coton Free School, Heath End Infant School and Chilvers Coton Infant School.

School Managers:
Lt. General Sir Edward Newdegate, Mr. Walter Pearson Evans, Reverend Robert Chadwick, Dr. Henry Thomas Tomlinson, Mr. Edward Ferdinand Melly.

Subscribers:
Paid before 30.9.1894

Sir Edward Newdegate	£10 Landowner, Arbury Hall
Griff Colliery	£10
James Knox	3 Guineas, Brickyard owner
Walter Pearson Evans	£3 Newdegate land agent
Thomas Kinder	£3 Grocer
Edward Melly	£1 Mine owner
Henry Tomlinson	£1 Doctor
Thomas Smith	£1 Builder
John B. Hall	£1 Chandler and Soap Merchant: Registrar
John ??? Gail	10/6
Frank Clay	10/6 Solicitor's clerk
Thomas E.Kershaw	10/- Mechanical Engineer
Edwin Peacock	10/6d Doctor
Henry Lewis	10/6d Commercial traveller
Joseph Towe	5/- Tailor [father of Florence Towe]
Joseph Bacon	5/- b.1851 Scripture Reader
J.H.Punter?	10/-
Miss Hall	3/- Probably Emma Hall, sister to John B. Hall above.
Mr Reader	3/6d

Appendix Eight:
Syllabus of work 1902. Arithmetic. An example of work pursued via the system of 'Standards'
[Standards 1 and 2 normally taught in the Infant School, 5-7 years]

Standard III	Simple rules/Compound money, Tables
Standard IV	Compound rules applied to weights and measures
Standard V	Fractions, Bills of parcels, Weights and measures
Standard VI	Decimals, Fractions, Common weights and measures
Standard VII	Averages, Vulgar Fractions/Decimals, Revision of Standard VI

On occasions pupils might be moved quickly through the standards or, alternatively, held back. The result would be a class with different ages all studying for the same standard or a teacher attempting to teach different standard at the same time to different girls or boys in the class. From 1876 children between 10 and 14 were normally required to stay at school until they had passed an examination in Standard four and obtained a labour certificate.

———•◆•———

Sources Used:

This is just a list of the most helpful sources among the many original documents and secondary sources used.

Warwickshire County Record Office Documents:
CR136/B3052 Lists of Sunday school and Free School Boys 1801-2.
CR136/B 5469-5595 Newdegate Correspondence, especially letters between Lady Elizabeth Newdigate and Sir Roger Newdigate, 1747-63.
CR136/C 1246 Draft of deed for settling a school at Chilvers Coton by Sir Roger Newdigate, 1765.
CR136/C3554-3571. Sir Roger Newdigate's will 1806, correspondence 1844-1898, plans 1864, 1891, 1894-5, statements about accommodation 1874 Report of meeting about Infant school 1881.
CR 136/V136 Expenditure of Sir Richard Newdigate's charity 1834-65.
CR136/ V156 Household Accounts 1747-1762.
CR136/ V175 Heath End and Chilvers Coton Schools' account Book 1844-87.
CR312/ 1-2 Chilvers Coton Girls' School log books 1875-1932, CR 312/5-8 Shepperton County Junior School logbooks 1874-1948.
CR 312/4 Logbook of Evening Continuation School, October 1893-March 1903.
CR320/1 Account book of Sir Roger Newdigate, 1757-63.
CR 1841/31 List of children in the Free School Chilvers Coton, 1746: poor children clothed, 1743-6.
CR 764/275 Chilvers Coton Sunday school rules and lists of children attending.
DR 374/105 Chilvers Coton Evening Continuation school minute book,1893-1903.
DR 374/99 List of Inhabitants of Chilvers Coton with children in respective families under 14, 1835.
DR 374/103 Subscription book for Chilvers Coton Free School, Heath End Infant School and Chilvers Coton, 1893-4.

———◆———

Census records for England and Wales, 1841-1911.
Nuneaton Miscellany files in Nuneaton Library, especially Volumes 6, 12, 15.
Nuneaton Chronicle.
Nuneaton Observer.
Chilvers Coton Heritage Centre – collection of materials.
Charity Commissioners Report on Chilvers Coton 1835 – House of Commons Papers Vol21 pt.2.
Wills from the National Archives, on line at Access to Archives: John Viall 1733, Edmund Dudley 1770.

Secondary Sources

Clark, George, The Old Rebel, A Life in Nuneaton 1885-1960 (2011)

Compton, Hugh J., The Oxford Canal London (1971).

Dent, H.C., Century of English Education (1970).

Digby, Anne and Searby, Peter, Children School and Society in 19th Century England (1981).

Gooder, Eileen, The Squire of Arbury (1990).

Gordon, Peter, The Victorian School Manager (1974).

Hurt, J.S., Elementary Schooling and the Working classes, 1860-1918 (1979).

Jones M.G., The Charity School Movement (2nd edition, 1974).

Laqueur, Thomas W., Religion and Respectability: Sunday Schools and Working-class Culture (1976).

McCann, Philip (ed.), Popular Education and Socialisation in the 19th Century (1977).

Neuburg, Victor E., Popular Education in 18th Century England (1971).

Paterson, David, Leeke's Legacy: a History of King Edward VI School Nuneaton (2011).

Silver, Pamela and Harold, The Education of the Poor: The History of a National School, 1824-1974 (1974).

Simon, Brian, The Two Nations and the Educational Structure, 1780-1870 (1974).

Smelser ,Neil J., Social Paralysis and Social change: British working class education in the 19th Century (1992).

Stephens, W.B., Education, Literacy and Society 1830-1870: the Geography of Diversity in Provincial England (1987).

Sutherland, Gillian, Policy making in Elementary Education, 1870-1895 (1973).

Vincent, David, Literacy and Popular Culture (1989).

Wardle, David, English Popular Education, 1780-1970 (1976).